Also by Raymond B. Flannery, Jr., Ph.D:

*Becoming Stress-Resistant
Through the Project SMART Program*

*Post-Traumatic Stress Disorder:
The Victim's Guide to Healing and Recovery*

*Violence in the Workplace*

*Violence in America: Coping with Drugs
Distressed Families, Inadequate Schooling, and Acts of Hate*

For Those Who Serve
Others in Need

# Contents

# Preface

Violence in the United States has been on the increase during the past thirty-five years, and is now a frequent and unwelcome visitor in our communities, in our worksites, and even in our own homes. Of the major crimes of homicide, robbery, rape, and assault, assault has seen the largest increment, a full six-fold increase during this thirty-five year period.

The potential negative effects on the victims of these crimes is considerable, and includes possible death, permanent disability, medical injury, medical and legal expense, lost productivity, and intense human suffering in the form of psychological trauma and untreated Posttraumatic Stress Disorder (PTSD).

Aggressive outbursts may occur at any time and in any place. Drive-by shootings on the street; domestic abuse in the home; and violence in worksites, such as in corporate/industrial, police/ corrections, emergency services, and school/college settings are daily events in our country. Health care settings have not been immune from these problems either as twenty-five years of published research indicates. While homicides and rapes do occur in health care facilities, the most frequent type of violence is that of patient assault on other patients or staff. In these instances, the patient and staff victims have had any medical injuries attended to, and the victims have received informal counseling from the staff. However, little of a systematic nature has been available for the psychological needs of staff victims in the aftermath of these assaults.

In late 1989, the management in one state mental hospital in the Massachusetts Department of Mental Health (DMH) decided to address the issue of patient assaults on staff in a systematic and supportive way for all employee victims. Because of my past and continuing interest in violence and its impact on victims, they requested my help in these matters.

In response to the needs of these assaulted employee victims, I developed the Assaulted Staff Action Program (ASAP). ASAP is a voluntary, systems-wide, peer-help, crisis intervention approach for addressing the psychological sequelae of patient assaults on staff. This approach includes individual crisis counseling, ward unit debriefings, a staff victims' support group, employee victims' family counseling, and professional referrals. ASAP has been associated with providing victims with needed support in times of crisis, and, in some facilities, with sharp reductions in the frequency of assaults within the facility.

These pages outline the steps necessary to design, field, and then maintain an ASAP program on an ongoing basis. Included are the standards of performance, clinical practice guidelines, basic training procedures, and all of the needed report forms. The book also outlines the problems and solutions that ASAP has encountered during its eight years of providing services. For these reasons, it is best to read the book as a whole first to understand how an ASAP program works. The reader can then return to individual chapters for help in creating an ASAP program specific to the needs of any individual facility.

The first chapter provides a detailed overview of violence. It is the reason that ASAP programs have been developed, and this chapter is provided for those who wish an updated review of this major national public health epidemic. This information is necessary for developing a sound ASAP program. A reader familiar with these matters, however, may wish to begin with chapter two and use the information in chapter one later on, when designing ASAP programs for specific institutional needs.

The ASAP approach is flexible and modular in design, and holds great promise for settings other than health care and for addressing the aftermath of violent acts besides assault. For example, community agencies could field an ASAP team for children who continually witness street violence, programs for battered women could provide ASAP for spouses and children, a college ASAP program could assist victims of date-rape, and there are many similar possibilities in corporate and industrial settings. The debriefing of tellers who have been victims of bank robberies is but one example of need. While patient assaults toward staff are used as the model for purposes of illustration in the book, the interested reader is encouraged to consider how an ASAP program could be created to address the psychological aftermath of violence for victims that they may encounter in their own particular settings. Toward that end, the chapters begin with vignettes of some act of violence in a variety of differing settings to stimulate thought.

The extent of violence in America is great. The psychological impact of this violence on the victims is painful. However, we are not helpless in the face of these events. ASAP is one helpful approach for these victims.

No book is ever fully written by one person. An author's roots are many and diverse. I would like to first thank Elaine Anderson, R.N., Kenneth Allen, R.N., Mary Barry, R.N., Kevin Brown, M.H.W., Margaret Corrigan, R.N., Joanne Cremins, R.N., Steven Foell, R.N., Douglas Hughes, R. N., Lisa Laudani, Louise Marks, L.I.C.S.W., Danielle Morgan, Brenda Peterson, M.H.W., Lenore Pollen, L.I.C.S.W., Virginia Stevens, R.N., Phyllis Stone, L.I.C.S.W., and Laurel Uzoma, R.N., the ASAP team leaders, and all of the over one-hundred-and-fifty ASAP team members who provide dedicated, voluntary, continuous service to their colleagues. All of us in ASAP also thank the employee victims, whom we have been honored to serve, for the many lessons that they have shared with us about violence and its impact on human functioning.

In addition, I would like to pay special thanks to the following persons who have provided important academic, clinical, or administrative support on behalf of the ASAP project presented in these pages: Paul Appelbaum, M.D., Paul Barreira, M.D., Joseph Coyle, M.D., Audrey DeLoffi, L.I.C.S.W., Robert Dorwart, M.D., George Everly, Jr., Ph.D., Paul Fulton, Ph.D., Charles Gallagher, M.Ed., Wallace Haley, Jr., M.D., Judith A. McNamara, Jeffrey T. Mitchell, Ph.D., Walter Penk, Ph.D., Mollie Schoenberg, Nancy R. Seeley, M.A., Virginia Stevens, R.N., Phyllis Stone, L.I.C.S.W., Marylou Sudders, L.I.C.S.W., Judith Tausch, R.N., Andrew Walker, and James Woods, S.J., Ed.D. I have been especially fortunate to have a highly talented production team in the production of this book: Caroline J. Zimmerman and Jason Lawrence at Chevron Publishing, Matthew Czapanskiy at the Image Mill, Inc.,

Norma Robbins, typist, and my wife, Georgina, who has served as librarian, researcher, and indexer for this manuscript. The counsel and advice of these men and women has been wise and helpful, but any errors remain my sole responsibility.

This book is dedicated to the men and women throughout the world who devote the days of their lives to the service of others in need.

Raymond B. Flannery, Jr., Ph.D., F.A.P.M.
Autumn, 1997

## Author's Note and Editorial Method

Violence in America is a rapidly expanding area of scientific and medical inquiry. Similarly, its impact in the form of psychological trauma and untreated Posttraumatic Stress Disorder (PTSD) is also being continuously examined with medicines and other forms of treatment that are constantly being upgraded and improved.

ASAP is one response to this need. Since ASAP is a clinical treatment intervention, ASAP programs should pay close attention to the clinical and administrative issues that are raised for consideration. Input from chief executive officers, counsel, human resources, medical directors, and other interested parties should be sought, and their advice and direction, followed. **Non-mental health organizations will need to consult a mental health professional who is trained in crisis intervention services about ASAP training, service delivery, and malpractice issues for their specific organizational needs.** In addition, ASAP programs are encouraged to incorporate any new relevant scientific findings, and to continuously monitor the quality of the services that they provide.

\* \* \* \* \*

All of the examples in this book are real events that have befallen victims of violence. Each has been disguised to protect the anonymity of those involved.

# ASAP REPORT FORMS

# ASAP REPORT FORMS (continued)

# PART 1

## THE ASSAULTED STAFF ACTION PROGRAM (ASAP): THEORY

# Chapter

# 1

## VIOLENCE IN AMERICA

*Never shall I forget those moments that murdered my God
And my soul, and turned my dreams to dust.*
- Elie Wiesel

*Look after him; and, if you spend any more, I will
repay you on my way back.*
- Luke, X, 30-35

Her eyes opened wide with excitement.

" . . . we are pleased to inform you that you have been selected for the position of overnight staff in our community residence . . ."

For as long as she could remember, Ellen had always wanted to serve others, to reduce suffering, to make the world a better place. Social work was her choice for these career goals, and, now that she has just completed college, this first job would provide her with needed experience for her graduate studies later on.

A staff of ten mental health counselors provided twenty-four-hour care for eight residents with serious mental illness. The patients were of both genders, all ages, and all social classes. Many had been victims of violence at the hands of others. For Ellen, the residence was an opportunity for observation, for study, and for kindness. It was she, as the overnight staff person, who would be there in the darkness of the night for the residents, the night when souls such as these were often troubled.

Her first four months had been demanding. Learning about diagnoses, medicines, and treatment plans was painstaking, but the work, especially the direct care of the patients, was deeply rewarding.

Pepper was Ellen's favorite.  Similar in age, Pepper was a young adult with schizophrenic illness, who often heard voices of persecution telling her to harm self or others.  Pepper was also burdened with memories of incest at the hands of her step-father, and she drank heavily to avoid the intrusiveness of both.

Before retiring for the night, Ellen thought about Pepper's behavior for the past two weeks.  Aimlessly riding the subways for hours at a time, pacing endlessly on the back porch.  Something was amiss.  Ellen would speak to the doctor in the morning.

At 5:30 A.M., there was a sudden knock on the door.  Ellen put on her robe, and opened the door to see Pepper lunge at her eyes with highheeled shoes . . . .

As Ellen lay in the intensive care unit awaiting emergency eye surgery, she felt frightened, bereft, and crushed in defeat.  In her bandaged darkness, her only companion was the beeping of her cardiac monitor.  If my heart breaks from sorrow and the monitor stops, she wondered silently, will I have to listen to the moment of my own death as well?

No one answered.

An act of violence.  Bodily injury.  Psychological terror.  Depression.  Dreams crushed.  Here it is a mental health counselor, but, in truth, it could have been any one of us.

Violence in America has been increasing during the past thirty-five years, and is now a frequent visitor in our homes, in our communities, and in our worksites.  Offices, classrooms, fast-food restaurants, playgrounds, and the like are no longer havens.  Violent acts such as those of homicide, terrorism, rape, robbery, and assault continue to stalk us each day. So pervasive has this level of violence become that most Americans now cite lack of personal safety as one of their primary causes of concern.  These fears are well-founded. *Violence in America has become a national public health problem.*

Among these acts of human aggression, assaults have seen the sharpest increase, a full six-fold increment (Flannery, 1997).  Consider the following:

- A teacher in an urban high school is assaulted as she attempts to stop a fight between two male students.

- A union member in a shipping company is punched by a nonunion member on the loading dock.

- A corrections officer is bitten by a prisoner in an inmate melee in the prison cafeteria.

- An emergency room nurse is kicked by an intoxicated patron who was himself lacerated in a barroom fight.

- A military recruit is sexually assaulted by her drill instructor in boot camp.

- Two hurried drivers begin to hit each other over who had the right of way at the intersection.

- A college sophomore is pinned to the ground in her dorm in an attempted rape by her date.

These and similar violent incidents exact an enormous toll on society. The impact of these events may result in death, permanent disability, medical injury, medical and legal expense, lost productivity, and human suffering in physical pain and in psychological trauma. This psychological trauma may evolve into Posttraumatic Stress Disorder (PTSD). If left untreated, PTSD with the full weight of its human misery may last until death.

What can victims do to deal effectively with this psychological aftermath of violence? What common options do Ellen and other victims have to put these painful events behind them and to get on with their lives?

One solution is to deny that the event really mattered or that its impact is of any consequence. In these cases, victims attempt to put the violent events out of mind. For example, a bus driver tells his shop steward that the assault by the angry passenger really did not hurt. Another common coping response is to accept the violence as part of the work as in the mental health worker who insists that violence comes with the turf. A third common strategy of victims is to blame themselves and withdraw in shame. For example, a rape victim may blame herself for being raped because she was wearing shorts at the time of the crime. Such self-blame provides an illusion of being in control.

All of these strategies are weak because the victims remain isolated from others, because they do not restore a sense of mastery to foster continued growth, and because they do not help the victims ascertain some reasonable explanation or meaning for why the event occurred. Untreated PTSD is a very real possibility in these cases.

A somewhat better solution is to speak to families, friends, or peers to help make sense out of what has happened. Here victims are not cut off from human support. However, the impact of traumatic events is complex and may impair feelings and thought processes. It is unlikely that well-intentioned families and friends will have the needed formal training for counseling victims of violence. Another somewhat more helpful approach is to seek professional counseling. However, such counseling by therapists especially trained in psychological trauma is often not readily available, or is more of a financial burden than the victim can bear.

There is another answer: *The Assaulted Staff Action Program (ASAP)*. It is a better answer because ASAP's sole purpose is to provide immediate victim debriefing by counselors trained in such matters.

*The Assaulted Staff Action Program* (ASAP; Flannery, 1995, 1997, 1998; Flannery, Fulton, Tausch, & DeLoffi, 1991; Flannery, Hanson, Penk, Flannery, & Gallagher, 1995; Flannery Penk, Hanson, & Flannery, 1996) is a voluntary, systems-wide, peer-help, crisis counseling intervention to assist employee victims in dealing with the psychological aftermath of patient assaults on staff. ASAP provides a range of crisis interventions for individual, group, and employee family needs. The ASAP program monitors any symptoms associated with psychological trauma and PTSD as well as any victim disruptions in the domains of personal mastery, caring attachments to others, and the ability to make meaningful sense of the violent event. ASAP provides needed support for victims at a difficult moment in their lives, and is, itself, sometimes associated with sharp reductions in subsequent levels of violence in the facilities in which it is fielded.

Let us return for a moment to Ellen, who is lying in the intensive care unit and awaiting emergency eye surgery. One of the most compelling aspects of this tragedy was that she was alone in her fear and depression. No one was there for her. No one answered.

What would have happened if an ASAP team had been there to reach out to her in this vulnerable moment?

First, the ASAP team member on-call would have been summoned by the residence staff, and would have gone to the intensive care unit. The team member would have sat quietly, and listened to Ellen describe her lonely ache. The team member would have begun the first steps needed to restore mastery and to make some sense of what happened. The ASAP team member would be the first caring attachment in Ellen's network, and would have sought to foster or restore additional support from others. Ellen would have been told about psychological trauma and its symptoms, and provided with basic strategies for coping with this sudden and overwhelming event. The same ASAP team member would have made arrangements to meet with Ellen as often as possible in the next few days and weeks. When the immediate crisis had passed, she would have been offered a support group for victims, if she wished it.

At the same time this was happening, additional ASAP team members would have been sent to the patients' residence. There, debriefings for any witnesses to the event would have taken place. This would be followed by a group debriefing for every resident and staff member in the house to address the turmoil and fear that such events generate. As with Ellen, offers of subsequent visits would be made.

Finally, outreach to Ellen's parents, family, or roommates would have been undertaken in an attempt to address the impact of this horrific event on the extended family and network of friends. Quiet, comprehensive, consistent, ASAP would be there to listen and to offer support in the darkness, until the matter was fully resolved.

These pages are about the ASAP program, and how to design, field, and maintain an ASAP program to help with the victim problems that a facility may need to address. Although ASAP was designed for assaulted health care providers, its comprehensive set of crisis intervention procedures are applicable to other types of violence and other types of settings, including community agencies coping with the aftermath of violence as well as the more formal settings of corporate/industrial, police/corrections, emergency services, and school/college facilities. While a state mental hospital health care setting is used in the book for purposes of illustration, the ASAP program is modular and flexible in design. The reader is encouraged to think about victim needs, where an ASAP team could make an important and helpful difference.

Since ASAP interventions are based on responses to violent acts, it is important that future ASAP team members have a basic understanding about the violence in our culture and why it occurs. Violence is why ASAP teams have come into being. Moreover, one important component of every ASAP debriefing is to help the victim to be able to make some meaningful sense of what appears to be a senseless act of human destructiveness. For most victims, understanding the nature of violence is an important factor in accepting what has happened and in moving on in life. An overview of violence assists the ASAP team member to be a more effective counselor in helping the victim to again establish a meaningful purpose for life.

Toward that end this chapter provides an overview of the nature and extent of violence in America. It includes:

- The nature and extent of violence,
- Types of potential assailants,
- The cause of violence,
- The impact of violence as psychological trauma, and
- Risk management strategies for addressing violence.

These are complex matters beyond the scope of this review. The interested reader is referred to Flannery (1995, 1997) for a more detailed analyses of these matters.

Joseph Conrad stated it most incisively. When we study violence, we journey deeper and deeper into the heart of darkness. Violence is always with us, and mourning in America is an ongoing process. To understand this adversary more fully, let us begin our inquiry into the heart of darkness.

## VIOLENCE IN AMERICA

### Its Nature and Extent

Although there are many differing, technical definitions of violence and crime, for our purposes we shall define violence as the intentional use of physical force to injure or intimidate another, and crime as the commission of an act forbidden by public law. Not all violence is criminal (e.g. self-defense), nor is all crime violent (e.g. embezzlement). Frequently, they overlap, but these working definitions provide us with needed guidelines to begin to measure human aggression toward others, violence which is unacceptable except in cases of self-defense.

Violent crime is recorded in two main data sets. The first is the Federal Bureau of Investigation's (FBI) Uniform Crime Report (UCR). The UCR counts crimes reported by individuals and businesses. The second data set is that of the Bureau of the Census' National Crime Victimization Survey (NCVS). The NCVS tabulates personal and household victimizations, but excludes fraud, drug, white-collar, and victimless crimes. The first is accurate in obtaining data on serious crimes, such as homicides. The second is probably more accurate in measuring the true levels of other violent crime in our society, since not all crimes are reported to the police.

However, estimating the level of violent crime in society by these two data sets is further compounded by the problem of underreporting. Some victims do not report crimes because they fear reprisal. Others do not come forward because they feel it will be of no use. Still others remain silent because they do not realize that they have been victims of a crime (e.g., date-rape in which both parties had been drinking). Thus, while there is better reporting of crime in recent years, it is still reasonable to assume that much of the violence in society remains underreported.

By any measure, even with these noted limitations, the level of violence in America is truly frightening. In addition to increases in the four major crimes of homicide, rape, robbery, and assault, there have been similar increases in the lesser crimes of forgery, fraud, embezzlement, stolen property, vandalism, vice, narcotic drugs, gambling, offenses against family and children, drunkenness, and drunken driving.

Table 1 presents the comparative crime rates in the United States for the four major types of offenses that cause the bulk of human suffering, physical pain, material loss, and psychological trauma. Table 1 presents these crime rates in 1960, a low crime period in our country's history, and in 1992, a high crime period. An inspection of the information in this table indicates staggering increases in all types of violent crime (Dobrin, Wiersema, Loftin, & McDowell, 1996). The homicide rate has doubled. The rates of rape and robbery have increased fivefold, and aggravated assault has grown by sixfold. Recent government reports have begun to reflect

# Table 1

**Rates of Major Crimes: 1960 and 1992:**

| Type of Crime | Victims* | |
| --- | --- | --- |
| | *1960* | *1992* |
| Homicide | 5.2 | 10.2 |
| Rape | 8.7 | 42.8 |
| Robbery | 49.6 | 263.6 |
| Aggravated Assault | 72.6 | 441.8 |

\* Rates per 100,000

modest declines in these rates of violent crime due to better policing, mandatory sentencing, and the like. It will be a hopeful sign if these initial declines continue. However, the sharp increases in crime since 1960 have been so great that the recent small declines in violence do not make us feel more safe as yet.

Recent crime data also reveal important information about the age and gender of today's assailants. There are sharp increases in crime by youth (ages fifteen to twenty-four) and by female youth assailants who are becoming as aggressive as their male counterparts (Flannery, 1997).

Finally, these crime data indicate the financial cost to society. Addressing violent crime requires about 550,000 federal, state, and municipal police, a private security force of one-and-a-half million employees, and the corrections costs to house all prisoners.

We do not feel safe because we are *not* safe.

# Table 2

## Types of Potential Assailants:

---

1. Average Citizens
2. Medically Ill Persons
3. Domestic Batterers
4. Disgruntled Employees
5. Juvenile Delinquents
6. Career Criminals

---

**Types of Potential Assailants**

Who is likely to commit these crimes? Table 2 lists the six most common categories of potential assailants (Flannery, 1995, 1997).

Average citizens, living in an age that values personal entitlement and material gain, comprise the first group. While their anger can be directed toward themselves, more commonly it is focused on others. Here are ordinary citizens who assault the bank mortgage officer, the bus driver, or the meter maid, when they do not obtain what they want. Overcome with anger, fear, jealousy or greed, they usually commit their crimes on impulse (actions without thought). Most never commit a second crime, and the courts deal with these matters by means of fines and probation.

Medically ill persons form the second group. Here are included individuals with medical conditions associated with violence and aggression such as serious mental illness, Organic Personality Syndrome, mental retardation, substance abuse, and similar medical problems. Depending on the circumstances, these assailants may or may not be held accountable for their crimes.

Domestic batterers form the third category of potential assailants. These perpetrators are usually male, have a past history of victimization at the hands of others, have a current history of substance abuse, have a basic fear of being rejected, and feel entitled to treat their family members as their own personal property.

Disgruntled employees make up the fourth group. Again, these assailants are more frequently male, are socially isolated, are often depressed, have a current history of substance abuse, and access to weapons. Their jobs come to mean everything to them so that the threat of job loss provokes violence in some.

Juvenile delinquents and career criminals form the last two categories. Delinquents are young, antisocial persons who are cruel to animals/people, and who are destructive of private property. They are often truant from school and ignore society's basic value of concern for others. Career criminals similarly fail to conform to society's norms. Aggressive behavior is common as they learn the skills necessary to commit the most heinous of crimes. They are motivated by the thrill of the chase, monetary rewards, and increases in power and influence.

### The Causes of Violence

When violence occurs, victims have a universal response in the form of a question: Why me? Why me is a plea for meaning, an attempt to understand why violence has befallen them. In addition to an awareness of the types of crimes and assailants, future ASAP team members also need a basic understanding of the possible causes of violence so that they can begin to help victims make meaningful sense of why these dreadful events have happened to them.

The theories of violence are found in four groupings: cultural, biological, sociological, and psychological (Flannery, 1997), and they are reviewed here briefly.

### *Cultural Theories*

Culture is defined as the customary beliefs, social structures, and material traits of a people. The culture through its societal institutions of business, government, families, schools, and religion teaches its members the social norms about how they are to interact with one another in helpful ways so that the general welfare of all is assured. Cooperation, self-restraint, patience, and concern for others are some of the more common values that many cultures espouse for their members so that a sense of community is sustained.

While there are evolutionary, conflict, and systems theories of culture, the structural-functional theory of Emile Durkheim (trans.

1951) appears the most helpful in understanding possible cultural sources of our current levels of violence. Durkheim believed that during periods of great social upheaval, the social norms in the basic societal institutions that we have noted above lose their regulatory force. Not only does the culture and its norms change, but the basic societal institutions themselves also change. In the absence of societal moral guidelines, individuals feel adrift and the sense of community is weakened. The tendency for social norms to lose their regulatory force is called *anomie*. The social disruptions that follow lead to increases in general distress, mental illness, suicide, and violent crime.

The United States is currently immersed in the type of major social evolution of which Durkheim spoke. Our country is moving from an industrial state that emphasized the manufacturing of products to a postindustrial state that is a knowledge-based society. The emerging world order emphasizes thinking, research, and discovery.

At the same time, our own country is moving toward participation in the global economy. In a global economy, citizens of all nations compete to sell their products and services with citizens from all corners of the earth. This competition enhances the need for producing the best quality products at the lowest cost, and subsequently increases the stress on individuals. We have seen the results of these two major changes in our own country in the form of downsizing, layoffs, and mergers.

This new world order has led to a three-tier division of our country's workforce. In the first tier are the knowledge workers. These are the individuals engaged in research and discovery in areas such as biotechnology, microelectronics, and health care. The second tier is comprised of the service workers who provide support to the first group. Here are included services such as banking, finance, real estate, transportation, communications, and utilities. The third tier is known as the permanent underclass, and is comprised of those workers who do not have the education and skills training to belong to one of the first two groups.

This shift toward the postindustrial state has occurred during the past thirty-five years, the same years as those of the sharp increases in violent crime that we examined earlier. This is what Durkheim's theory of anomie would predict. As the country goes through this major social upheaval, the sense of community is greatly weakened, and the major societal institutions that should provide us with the needed social norms for cooperative behavior are themselves undergoing change. The result is sharp increases in violence in the absence of a sense of community. This violence is particularly likely to occur in the permanent underclass, whose skills do not permit them more socially sanctioned ways to support themselves and their families. The country's moral compass becomes adrift.

*Biological Theories*

"It's a jungle out there." "Kill or be killed." "It's survival of the fittest." Expressions such as these reflect the intense pressure felt by many in today's age, and have raised the question of whether or not humans are born with a biological instinct to behave aggressively. A large body of data from ethnology and genetics (Flannery, 1997) indicates that there is no current evidence to suggest that humans are born to behave aggressively, except in cases of self-defense in the face of imminent harm. Some individuals may be born with characteristics that make aggressive behavior somewhat more likely, such as impulsivity, poor attention span, hyperactivity, or sensation-seeking behavior. Notwithstanding, many individuals have these characteristics and do not behave in aggressive and violent ways. Thus, humans do not appear to be born to behave in aggressive ways.

An examination of medical disorders, however, does indicate some biologically-based illnesses that may result in violent outbursts. Injuries to the cortex, the part of the brain involved in planning and problem-solving, may result in biological injuries that lead to aggressive behavior. Car accidents involving head injuries, severe cases of domestic battery, and athletic head injuries are examples of possible ways that the cortex could be damaged. Similarly, injuries to the limbic system can result in violence. The limbic system is a small part of the brain where feeling states are added to experience. Injuries to the brain in this area can result in hyperreactivity to routine events, and lead to impulsive hostility in some.

In addition to demonstrable brain injury cases, there are several medical conditions without clear brain injury, that are associated with the potential for aggressive outbursts. Common examples include mental retardation, Attention Deficit/Hyperactivity Disorder, serious mental illness, intermittent explosive disorder,

Organic Personality Syndrome, temporal lobe epilepsy, untreated PTSD, alcohol/drug abuse, depression/suicide, dementia, conduct disorders, antisocial personality disorders, borderline personality disorders, and paranoid personality disorders. [See Flannery (1995, 1997) for a detailed explanation of these medical conditions and their possible mechanisms that appear to contribute to violence.]

Do these biological problems confirm the common belief that, when individuals behave violently, they are not in their right minds? Not really. First, these medical conditions are rare, and could not in and of themselves account for the large increases in crime that we have noted. Second, there are good treatments for most of these illnesses. Thus, a person with one of these disorders might not be held accountable for his or her violent outburst the first time, if it was undiagnosed and untreated. However, after proper diagnosis and treatment, that person would most likely be held responsible subsequently, if he or she disregarded the treatment and became violent again. In most cases, an individual is freely choosing to behave in aggressive ways.

*Sociological Theories*

The sociological factors associated with violence and crime are familiar to us, since they are frequently reported in the media. They include poverty, inadequate schooling, discrimination, domestic abuse, substance abuse/easily available weapons, and the media themselves.

In many ways, poverty is the source of much violence. Individuals and families need adequate income for the basics in life, such as food, clothing, and shelter. Persons with disease, disability, lack of education, or blocked opportunity are frequently poor. The problem of poverty is becoming further compounded in our own age by the emergence of the postindustrial state. Men and women who were able to support themselves with marginal skills are now unable to find employment. To ensure survival, they turn to illegitimate means to acquire basic needs. Drug dealing is a common example, where the selling of drugs becomes a means of obtaining needed income.

Inadequate schooling makes such matters worse. As we enter the complexity of the postindustrial state with its emphasis on knowledge, many of our schools are failing to prepare the young for this new world order.  Buildings in physical disrepair, inadequate staffing, and inadequate supplies do not prepare students with the skills needed to cope in the postindustrial state.  Crime often follows.

Discrimination forms the basis for acts of hate committed against innocent fellow citizens who are singled out for some aspect of their personhood such as race, ethnicity, age, gender, sexual preference, religious beliefs, or medical or psychiatric disability. Citizens who are angry with their own inadequacies or who are unable to compete in the postindustrial state often direct this anger and rage towards persons who differ in one of the characteristics that we have just enumerated.

Domestic abuse is violence directed toward family members, and includes spousal abuse, child abuse, abuse by blood relatives, and abuse by step-relatives.  Domestic violence is aggression by definition, and includes all forms of physical abuse and sexual abuse, including marital rape and incest, as well as neglect, where the basic needs of the family's children for nurturance and survival are not provided by the adults.  In addition to the immediate danger from this violence in the home, the family members are learning that violence is a solution to solving conflicts and attaining one's goals.  This learning results in the intergenerational transfer of violence, so that subsequent generations encounter the same domestic violence (Widom, 1992).

Substance abuse, including the use of alcohol, is on the increase in our society.  These drugs disinhibit the cortical control centers in the brain so that the intoxicated person is more prone to be aggressive, when confronted.  At the same time, the drug culture that supplies these substances is arming itself with easily available weapons that can be purchased illegally on the street for less cost than the price of a pair of shoes.  These weapons are used in the turf wars over the markets for drug sales, but they also lead to a situation in which everyone involved is armed for purposes of self-defense. The result is a culture that has more firepower than the police, and that leads non-drug involved teenagers, among others, to arm themselves for self-protection.  Violence follows.

Finally, the media are implicated in society's increasing level of violence.  The programming in many media, especially music and television, use themes of exploitive sex and aggression to attract listeners.  Such programming rarely shows the long-term consequences of aggression, such as grieving parents, long-term disabilities, and the life-long consequences of untreated PTSD. Many in the viewing audience are seduced by the glamour and sense of invincibility. This violence does appear to lead to increased violence in some children. However, not all children who are exposed to violence in the media become violent. This process is complicated, and the interested viewer is referred to Wekesser (1995).

*Psychological Theories*

The final category of factors associated with violence are those that are psychological in nature. Humans have the capacity to assign meaning to events. For example, if Henry bumps into John in the hallway and John assumes it was accidental, little is likely to come from it. However, if John assumes that Henry did this on purpose, verbal or physical hostility may follow. In these cases, John is assigning different meanings to the same event.

In like manner, research has shown that there are common values and attitudes utilized by aggressive people in making meaning of events. These include the catharsis of feelings of anger and rage, and generating excitement through planning and implementing criminal behavior. Seeking justice for some perceived wrong by being both judge and jury, and self-indulgence in the belief that one is entitled to use violence to attain one's goals are two additional common methods of assigning faulty mastery. To these we could add religious/political beliefs, social acceptance by one's criminal peers, and even the sense of shame, in those cases where the aggressors believe that they are damaged goods or a disgrace to society because of past personal events in their own lives. Many feel that they must be punished.

The cultural, biological, sociological, and psychological factors that may increase the probability of violence occurring are summarized in table 3.

They are known as risk factors because their presence increases the likelihood of violence. It should be clearly understood that, with the exceptions of a few medical illnesses, acts of violence are freely chosen. Perpetrators of violence are in their right minds. They act impulsively or with premeditation, and courts hold such persons responsible for their behaviors. Not everyone with the risk

# Table 3

## Risk Factors for Violence:

*Cultural:*

Anomie

*Biological:*

Brain Injuries
Certain Medical Conditions

*Sociological:*

Poverty
Inadequate Schooling
Discrimination
Domestic Abuse
Substance Abuse/Easily Available Weapons
The Media

*Psychological:*

Catharis
Excitement
Seeking Justice
Self-Indulgence
Religious/Political Beliefs
Social Acceptance
Shame

factors becomes violent, however, so let us conclude this review of the risk factors with a helpful rule of thumb: the greater the number of risk factors present at any one time, the greater the likelihood that violence or crime may follow.

Regardless of which risk factor(s) leads to violence, the impact on the victim usually produces disruptions in day-to-day functioning, and great emotional distress, including psychological trauma. [See Flannery (1992, 1994) for a detailed discussion of psychological trauma and its consequences.] Since ASAP programs exist primarily to help victims cope with the psychological sequelae of traumatic events, as we have noted, we turn our attention to these matters next.

## PSYCHOLOGICAL TRAUMA: ITS AFTERMATH

### Psychological Trauma

Psychological trauma is a person's physical and psychological response to a sudden, unexpected, terrifying, potentially life-threatening event over which the person has no control. This state can be induced by being the direct victim of a violent event or by witnessing these dreadful events happening to others. Those who witness such events are, perhaps, best thought of as unrecognized victims. Even though direct victims receive the immediate attention of police and health care, the psychological impact on witness victims to these events may be just as disruptive as it is for actual victims. This possible impact is often overlooked by both the witnesses themselves, as well as the onsite emergency services and health care providers. Witnessing a colleague being assaulted, and observing dead and mutilated bodies as one provides emergency services are common examples of ways in which persons may become unrecognized victims.

Whether direct victim or witness victims, when the traumatic event happens, victims are at first stunned, then very frightened and then angry as they attempt to respond to the event. Heart and lungs are energized, muscles tighten for quick escape, and concentration and memory are focused intensely on finding a solution for ensuring survival. During this immediate crisis period, reasonable mastery, caring attachments, and some meaningful sense about what is happening may be disrupted. Hypervigilance, sleep disturbance, and repeated intrusive memories of the event may be present. Withdrawal from others may also follow (Everly & Lating, 1995).

This period of crisis may last from a few hours or days to as long as a month. Gradually the confusion and terror lessen, the victim returns to some semblance of daily routine, and the traumatic event begins to fade. But not always.

*Posttraumatic Stress Disorder (PTSD).* For some victims, the psychological distress continues and their lives remain disorganized. The symptoms remain. The disruptions in mastery, attachment, and meaning remain. This continuing impact after a month's time is known as PTSD, and it has two phases: The *acute/protest phase* and the *chronic/numbing phase.*

The *acute/protest phase* is characterized by anger and attempts to seek redress. These latter may include pressing charges, filing insurance claims, filing lawsuits, and even thoughts of revenge. The simple tasks of everyday life seem overwhelming and inconsequential, and the hypervigilance, sleep disturbances, and intrusive memories of the traumatic event remain. Much of this continuing anger is due to the body's output of adrenaline.

After six or seven months, the body can no longer sustain such increased output, and the victim enters the *chronic/numbing phase* of PTSD. During this period, the victim psychologically withdraws from many of life's activities. There is less behavior as the person avoids reminders of the traumatic event, and withdraws from other daily, nontraumatic activities, such as work, family, and community activities. There is less cognitive activity as the victim remains preoccupied with the traumatic event. There is usually less of a range of feeling states. Happiness, joy, pleasure are basically absent, and a state of low grade depression or numbness, intermittently interrupted by outbursts of anger and hostility, settle in. Disruptions in reasonable mastery, caring attachments to others, and in how to make meaningful sense of the violent event remain. The vigorous, active person has become a distressed and depressed victim. If left untreated, the disruptions of the *chronic/numbing phase* may last until death.

**Symptoms of Psychological Trauma**

Like most other medical conditions, psychological trauma and PTSD have symptoms, or signals to the person, that things are not right. In psychological trauma and PTSD conditions, symptoms are grouped into three different types: physical, intrusive, and avoidant. The most common and frequently occurring symptoms are listed in table 4.

# Table 4

**Common Symptoms in Psychological Trauma and PTSD:**

---

*Physical Symptoms:*

Hypervigilance
Exaggerated Startle Response
Sleep Disturbance
Difficulty with Concentration and Memory
Mood Instability, especially Anger and Depression

*Intrusive Symptoms:*

Recurring, Distressing Recollections (Thoughts,
    Memories, Dreams, Nightmares, Flashbacks)
Physical or Psychological Distress at an Event that
    Symbolizes the Trauma
Grief or Survivor Guilt

*Avoidant Symptoms:*

Avoiding Specific Thoughts, Feelings, Activities,
    or Situations related to the Trauma
Diminished Interest in Significant Activities
Restricted Range of Emotions/Psychological
    Numbness

---

*Physical Symptoms*

Physical symptoms arise from the body's physiological response to the crisis. Adrenaline is released into the body. It is converted to epinephrine in the body, and mobilizes the heart, lungs, and muscles to cope with the crisis. Adrenaline is also converted to norepinephrine in the brain, and creates a similar state of preparedness in the form of alert cognitive vigilance.

The continuous presence of adrenaline in the victim may lead to states of hypervigilance, exaggerated startle response, disturbed sleep, difficulty in concentrating and in remembering events, and periodic episodes of anger and depression.

The continuous presence of adrenaline in the brain in the form of norepinephrine produces an additional problem for many victims. It is known as *kindling,* a condition in which the continuous presence of norepinephrine has sensitized the delicate nerve fibers in the limbic system. Since this part of the brain is associated with feeling states, this process of sensitization results in small amounts of subsequent norepinephrine that produce PTSD symptoms as intense as those of the original traumatic event.

*Intrusive Symptoms*

If this state of sustained vigilance were not difficult enough, victims are also bothered by recollections of the violent event. It appears that this is the mind's way of having the person remember and process the event, so that the person will be able to cope more effectively, should violence happen again. Thoughts, memories, dreams, and nightmares are all examples of intrusive memories common to victims after the event.

One unique form of intrusive memory is that of a *flashback.* When an individual is attacked, the individual's brain has a remarkable capacity to ensure survival. When faced with an overwhelming event, the brain prevents itself from being overwhelmed by incapacitating detail in order that it may concentrate on survival. The brain allows the victim to put unnecessary painful details of the event out of memory temporarily so that the victim can focus entirely on safety. These unnecessary memory details are dissociated from present consciousness. They are stored in memory, where they have their own feelings, behaviors, and thoughts.

For example, three soldiers are in a foxhole during a live fire-fight. Their position takes a direct hit, and two of the three are killed. The surviving soldier sees the body parts of his two comrades strewn about the field. Through the process of dissociation, he is able to put these painful, but immediately unnecessary, details aside so that he is able to get back to safety behind his own lines.

After the crisis has passed, the brain will experience these intrusive memories as it attempts to heal itself by permitting the soldier to review these previously dissociated materials to foster more adaptive coping with any later violence. This re-experience of the dissociated material is known as a flashback. Since by anyone's standards, these flashback recollections are painful, many victims learn to put them out of conscious memory and back into the dissociated memory state. While this process brings some short-term relief, the presence of untreated, unintegrated dissociative memories may result in untreated PTSD over the longer term.

Two additional intrusive symptoms are symbolic reminders of the traumatic event and grief. Symbolic reminders are events or situations that remind the victim of the original traumatic situation, and may elicit the symptoms of physical arousal, especially fear and hypervigilance, as well as painful reminders of the original violence. For example, in the case noted above, parades with military units on holidays may remind the surviving soldier of his experiences in the foxhole. Grief is the final common intrusive memory. All trauma involves loss of some form, and all loss entails grieving. Grief (including survivor guilt, which is a form of grieving) reminds us of what we have lost, and provides a way of maintaining a sense of community with the deceased and a method of honoring their memory. Grieving is generally resolved within a reasonable period of time. If victims experience difficulty in grieving or refuse to grieve, untreated PTSD may again be an outcome.

*Avoidant Symptoms*

The presence of states of hypervigilance and continuously recurring memories of painful events is unpleasant, to say the least, and victims do what they can to distance themselves from these painful events.

First, they frequently avoid the place where the traumatic event occurred. They avoid the corridor where the rape took place, they transfer to another bank branch to avoid the memories of the robbery, and the like. The presence of these symbolic reminders of the traumatic events may produce the kindling phenomenon, and victims avoid these reminders that may result in PTSD symptomatology.

Similarly, everyday activities like athletics, dancing, even strenuous housework, may produce similar small increments in

adrenaline, and again through kindling produce intense PTSD
symptoms. Because of this continuing untreated distress, victims
avoid not only the scene of the violence, but may also avoid sports,
crowds, friends, promotions, and similar events that normally make
life enjoyable. Victims become depressed and numb. Life has no joy,
and there is no peace of mind.

**Psychological Disruptions in Psychological Trauma**
Just as violent events may result in distressing symptoms in
victims, the cardinal makers of good physical and mental health —
reasonable mastery, caring attachments, and a meaningful purpose in
life — may also be disrupted.

*Faulty Mastery*
By definition, reasonable mastery, or the ability to shape the
environment to meet our needs, may be disrupted in traumatic events.
The victim has no power to control the event, no matter how hard the
victim tries. While some victims are able to restore a reasonable
sense of mastery in short order, many are not.
Some compensate by assuming a stance of over-control.
Having lived through one traumatic event, the victim never wants to
feel totally out of control again. These victims try to control every
detail of their daily lives, no matter how large or small, pleasant or
unpleasant. Their goal is to plan every event in advance to avoid
being caught off guard. This strategy ultimately fails, since no
person can control every aspect of life. Unfortunately, these failed
attempts at control often lead these victims to re-double efforts at
constant vigilance, and the self-defeating cycle continues.
A second strategy to regain control is to blame oneself for
what has happened. Instead of accepting the fact that the person was
a victim of a crime or was the wrong person in the wrong place at the
wrong time, some persons create explanations for why they are at
fault. "If I had been more alert, my child wouldn't have been hit in
the drive-by shooting." "If I hadn't crossed the alley at dusk, I
wouldn't have been mugged." Statements such as these imply that
the victims have a plausible explanation for the violence, and, by
implication, can behave differently in the future and avoid
subsequent victimization. Self-blame provides the illusion of control,
and, like the approach of over-control, does not fit the facts of violent

behavior by others.

A third common approach to faulty mastery is to go to the other extreme of over-control and learn to be helpless. In these cases, victims who correctly perceived that they were not in control during the traumatic event, falsely assume that, because they were unable to control one situation, that they are unable to control any situation. This may include work, child-bearing, marriage responsibilities, friendships, or community tasks. In making the false generalization from the traumatic event to all events, victims learn to be helpless, and mastery is not restored.

A fourth inadequate solution to disrupted mastery is to use drugs or alcohol to calm one's nerves. While substance use may relieve the immediate physiological aftermath of a traumatic event, it precludes normal recovery in several ways. First, the victim now has additional chemicals in a nervous system already in disequilibrium from the violence. This may complicate normal physiological recovery. Second, the victim has learned an inadequate solution to the event. Victims' nerves will become frayed again as the substance loses its potency. Third, victims will likely reach for the substance again and increase the possibility of developing an addiction. Fourth, all of this takes needed time from the recovery process.

*Inadequate Attachments*

Violent events disrupt our caring attachments to others in at least two important ways.

The first is for victims to make avoidance responses to the presence of others. While some of this withdrawal is due to physical and intrusive symptoms, as we have seen, some of it is also an attempt to avoid others outright. To be a victim at the hands of others is to experience a powerful sense of mistrust of, and fear of, dependence on others. In violent circumstances, humankind does not seem caring and supportive, and withdrawal from others is a protective mechanism to avoid further injury and harm. All of this is further complicated, if the victim was socially isolated to begin with.

The second negative impact from traumatic events is the withdrawal of others. Violence is frightening and we seek to avoid it, if we can. This includes those whom it has touched. Friends, loved ones, neighbors may complicate the avoidance process by victim-blaming. This creates the illusion of control in non-victims in the same way that self-blame provides the illusion of control in victims. For example, if one blames Jane for being mugged because she walked in the park at dusk, one assumes that one would not do this, and, thus, be safe from harm.

The interaction of this joint psychological withdrawal by both parties at the very time a caring support network is needed greatly impedes the recovery of many victims.

*Faulty Meaning*

Violence destroys the victim's sense of the world as a safe, predictable environment that is worthy of one's investment of time and energy. Victims do their best to cope, but the ugliness of an act of violence colors their perceptions and sense of perspective (Horowitz, 1976). Victims continue to feel unsafe in ways that they do not understand. Some fear that the event will happen again. Some are afraid of their own anger, and fear that they will strike out against others in the same way that they have been victimized. Still others experience shame, because they feel that they should have been able to cope more adequately.

Victims who experience these conflictual states are unable to understand the principles of nature that govern natural or man-made disasters due to structural failure. Nor do they understand the deliberate evil acts freely chosen by twisted human minds. Recovery is impeded until the victim is successful in searching for the soul of goodness in things evil.

## Consequences of Untreated Psychological Trauma

If the acute symptoms of psychological trauma and its disruptions in mastery, attachment, and meaning do not pass within a reasonable period of time or are not adequately treated, several types of unwanted psychological sequelae may ensue. Three common outcomes are anxiety states, depressive states, and substance abuse.

*Anxiety States*

In addition to hypervigilance and general psychological ill-ease, certain other types of anxiety states may develop. Panic is one. Panic is a state of terrifying fear that comes upon a person suddenly and for no discernible reason. While some forms of panic may be genetic or related to depression, in other cases these states of panic may be induced by incorrect statements that victims make to themselves. Victims may become frightened, and then make statements such as "I am losing my mind" or "I am going to have a fatal heart attack right now." These statements are inaccurate, but are still capable of producing chest pain, choking sensations, trembling, fears of dying, fears of the world going dark, or of going completely out of control, symptoms some victims incorrectly interpret as panic.

Somatoform disorders are another way victims may communicate their distress nonverbally. In somatoform disorders, the person's psychological distress is expressed in bodily experiences rather than in conscious thought or feelings. Sudden paralysis with no known medical cause, asthmatic attacks, irritable bowel syndrome, and dermatologic problems may occur in some victims. Chronic pain is yet another example. Here victims may be expressing their psychological pain by displacing it to body pain, such as the neck, head, shoulders, or lower back.

While there are many possible medical causes for some anxiety states, sudden onset of anxiety states after traumatic events should raise the question of the traumatic event as possibly being part of the etiology.

*Depression*

Depression is marked by a loss of energy, a loss of interest in daily activities, a loss of libido, and feelings of sadness, anger, guilt, and/or hopelessness.

While some forms of depression appear to be produced by genetic illnesses, depression can be caused by other factors as well. Depression can be precipitated in normal persons when they experience a loss. The loss can be through the death of loved ones; through acts of violence such as battery and rape where one loses one's physical integrity; or through witnessing harmful events happening to others, which leads to a loss of innocence about the world. Contemplating man's inhumanity to man in all of its perverse shapes is depressing in itself.

There is an additional way in which victims can become depressed. When victims are in a state of sustained physiological arousal, the brain utilizes norepinephrine, as we have seen. For this chemical to work most effectively, an additional chemical, serotonin, is present and acts as a catalyst to ensure that norepinephrine works properly. However, serotonin is one of the chemicals in the brain that makes us feel good. When it acts as a catalyst, it is depleted, and, when it is depleted, victims feel depressed.

This chemical depression may interact with the depression due to the psychological loss, and severely impair a victim's capacity to respond. In some cases, suicidal thoughts and behaviors may also be present. Depressed victims, including witness victims, should always be taken seriously.

*Substance Abuse*

Victims often attempt to self-medicate the distressing symptoms of psychological trauma and PTSD with drugs and alcohol.

Psychiatrist Edward Khantzian (1985) has a theory that certain drugs are used to soothe painful feeling states in persons with substance abuse. Having completed several assessments of substance abusing persons myself, and, having found histories of violence in most, I would take Dr. Khantzian's theory one step further, and postulate that many of these painful feelings are the direct result of untreated PTSD.

Table 5 summarizes Dr. Khantzian's main findings. Amphetamines (including diet pills) and cocaine and crack are used to self-medicate feelings of depression. Alcohol and barbiturates (sedatives) are used to dampen anxiety states, and opiates appear to be taken to relieve anger and rage. Persons who have one drug of choice are most often self-medicating the painful feeling state noted in table 5.

In our culture, alcohol is the most prevalent drug of choice. A person is defined as drinking alcoholically, if the person's drinking gets him or her into trouble. These troubles can arise at work, at home, with the children, with one's friends, or when driving while intoxicated. It does not matter what type of alcoholic beverage is consumed, how much is consumed, or where it is consumed. If the alcohol gets the person in trouble, then that person is drinking alcoholically.

In our clinics, we have four questions that we use to help people learn whether or not they have problems with alcohol. (1) Do you need an eye-opener? (2) Do you get angry when people discuss

# Table 5

## Substance Abuse and Self-Medication:

| Type of Substance | Type of Psychological Distress |
|---|---|
| Amphetamines Cocaine | Depression |
| Alcohol Barbiturates | Anxiety |
| Opiates | Anger/Rage |

alcohol? (3) Has anyone ever told you to cut back on your consumption? (4) Do you feel guilty about your drinking? An answer of "yes" to two or more of these questions indicates a problem with alcohol.

There are other health consequences from untreated psychological trauma and PTSD (Flannery, 1992, 1994) in addition to these three. All of them should serve to alert us to the importance of treating the victims of psychological trauma early on to prevent such unnecessary additional human suffering.

### ADDRESSING VIOLENCE IN AMERICA

Given the nature and extent of violence in America and its deadening impact on the mind in the form of psychological trauma, what advice might future ASAP team members provide to victims and their organizations, if they were asked for useful suggestions to prevent future episodes of violence? These are complex matters (Flannery, 1995, 1997), but there are some practical suggestions that ASAP members could outline.

First, the problem of denial needs to be addressed. A good

deal of crime and violence in our country happens because many of us do not believe that these things can happen to us. They can and they do. Therefore, an early suggestion to victims and organizations is to fully understand that anyone can be victimized, and that everyone should take sensible precautions to reduce unreasonable risks. Full prevention of violence is unlikely at this period in our history, but there are many things that individuals can do to contain and reduce the chances of violent and criminal events from occurring. Denial keeps us from considering possible sensible precautions.

Second, we can and should implement some of the basic strategies and technologies that are available currently to increase safety. There is a large selection of security systems for home and office to regulate access and to monitor the premises on an ongoing basis, if there is this need. Similarly, there are many opportunities to learn differing systems of self-defense. All of us need to learn the warning signs of impending loss of control, and strategies to escape or to contain whatever type of criminal or violent behavior that we may encounter. Stress management strategies are also of assistance in that we can train ourselves to remain relatively calm in case of violence. In this way we enhance our chances of thinking clearly at a moment of crisis, and of behaving in ways that decrease the possibility of death and injury. These stress management techniques have the additional advantage of improving the general, overall quality of our lives.

Having noted the immediate safeguards each of us can put in place individually, collectively we need to focus on the third pathway to reducing violence. This includes restoring and strengthening the sense of community, and requires the efforts of business, government, families, schools, and religion. As a society, we need to strengthen the caring attachments that we need to have with each other. Our current national values that overemphasize the primacy of self, material goods, and immediate gratification need to be balanced by a concern for the welfare of others. While we do have an emphasis on human rights, the sense of responsibility toward others in the exercise of these rights is frequently minimized.

In addition to the general strengthening of community, society needs to address the sociological risk factors that are currently contributing to our high levels of violence. Poverty, especially in its new format of the permanent underclass, breeds crime and violence, and society needs to assist poor people with adequate opportunities for employment and housing. Improving our schools is one place to begin. The country needs to agree on some form of basic national standards for high school graduation, and then to provide the curriculum and support services needed to attain these goals.

There are similar needs for citizen education and improved law in the areas of discrimination, domestic abuse, substance abuse, and the media. Although our society expects us to demonstrate concern for one another, these ongoing problems fester in the social fabric and often result in violence. For example, we have seen how children who witness violence between their parents at home may themselves resort to violence in their own marriages later on. This is true, even if they were never direct victims of violence themselves. Recent police approaches that have included the arrest and conviction of domestic batterers bring about sharp reductions in subsequent violence (Bouza, 1990). We are not helpless in the face of this violence, but, as our national statistics suggest, much remains to be done.

The ASAP program can be an important approach in addressing violence in its own right. We have noted how some victims of untreated psychological trauma and PTSD may themselves be prone to subsequent aggressive outbursts. We have also seen how caring attachments, the victim's sense of community, may be disrupted by traumatic events. ASAP addresses both of these issues, and has been associated with reductions in the frequency of assaults in some facilities.

Perhaps, most importantly, ASAP programs address the most fundamental cause of our present levels of violence, the lack of community, the anomie described by Durkheim (trans.1951). ASAP programs not only create a sense of support for individual victims, but they also create improved morale and a caring worksite community. ASAP's verbal and nonverbal presence throughout each facility provides a strong message that no one is alone in the face of violence. To the extent that anomie may exist in a facility, the presence of an ASAP team can serve to mitigate its potential negative impact. Thus, ASAP not only addresses the aftermath of violence, but is itself a strategy for reducing the risk of such violence in the first place.

This concludes our short review of violence in America. It has included a discussion of the nature and types of violence, its sharp increase in recent years, the initial profiles of the major types of assailants, some of the more common factors thought to be causative in such events, and how these might be addressed.

Similarly, we have reviewed the important basic components of psychological trauma and PTSD. We have noted the various types of symptoms associated with these two medical conditions as well as the disruptions of reasonable mastery, caring attachments to others, and a meaningful purpose in life, and how these may impair human functioning.

This review illustrates how ASAP has evolved to address the needs of health care staff assaulted by patients, and it also demonstrates how an ASAP program could be readily employed in other types of settings.

Hopefully, with this body of information we now have a better understanding of the distress that Ellen must be experiencing as she lies in the intensive care unit and awaits her emergency surgery, and begin to answer her question: Why me?

With this overview of violence and psychological trauma as background, we are now ready to examine in detail the ASAP intervention program that could be a first response to Ellen and to other victims. We start at the beginning and explore how ASAP came to be.

# Chapter

# 2

## THE ASSAULTED STAFF ACTION PROGRAM (ASAP)

*An injury to one is the concern of all.*
- Knights of Labor Motto

*Speak that I may know you.*
- Ben Johnson

The flash of fuchsia.

It was April 29th. He knew that because he had not slept on April 28th for the past fifteen years.

He sat quietly on the bar stool and nursed a drink. How would he handle his daughter's wedding in three days? He wondered about that. He would get to be father of the bride but once, and he wanted everything to go well. The plans were in place, but he remained apprehensive. She was both his greatest joy and his most intense dread.

It was fifteen years ago, but the flash of fuchsia was as present now as his own breath. Perhaps it was fitting that the sun never rose on the dark streets of his city.

A modest family man, Henry had spent twenty-nine years as a subway motorman beneath the streets of the city to care for his wife and to ensure that his daughter's life would be better than their own. The tedium, the stale air, the incessant noise, the monotony of almost three decades of darkness were fraught with meaning as his daughter's wedding neared.

As he sat on the stool, he thought back yet again to why they had stood at the edge. As the four car train approached the platform, several passengers were crowded too closely near the edge. The young girl in the fuchsia jacket was especially at risk. He sounded the warning horn.

In an instant, a flash of fuchsia before his windshield. Cries of horror from the platform. The hiss of pneumatic steam. Screeching brakes. The sudden shudder beneath the train's wheels as tempered steel crushed bone, cartilage, and sinew. A disquieting silence.

The head and blood of the young girl, his daughter's age, lay beside the electrified third rail . . .

The coroner termed it suicide. The transit authority gave him two days to rest.

At his request, his daughter had never worn the color fuchsia.

Three days hence would be her wedding day, but in the dark night of his soul it would always be April 28th.

Henry is an example of a victim of violence attempting to cope with the untreated psychological sequelae of this painful event. His intrusive memories; his distance from others, including his own daughter; his inability to make sense of why it happened, even fifteen years later; and his self-medication of this traumatic distress with alcohol are constant reminders of the untold tale of this sad, angry, suicidal young citizen. Was she angry with the transit system? With a culture that emphasizes material goods? We will never know, since she directed her anger toward herself, and the answers to these questions were silenced with her death. We do know, however, that Henry is still attempting to cope with her act of depression and rage.

There are many Henrys, victims of violent events, who have not received proper treatment. It is estimated that anywhere from five percent to fifteen percent of victims of various types of traumatic events (Caldwell, 1992; Norris, 1992) do not receive needed care and go on to develop untreated PTSD.

As we have seen, denial and avoidance are not helpful ways to deal with the aftermath of violent events, so Henry and other victims might seek more suitable help in the form of professional counseling from individual therapists trained in the complexities of psychological trauma, or in the form of an organizational trauma response team, such as ASAP.

In truth, if these victims had sought assistance from an organizational trauma debriefing team before 1975, they would not have fared very well at all with their request. While systematic organizational debriefing teams are effective, as we shall see, they are a relatively recent development in the field of counseling.

While the military had long known that some soldiers exposed to live combat might be adversely affected mentally, there were few successful treatments for psychological trauma, or "shell-shock," as it was known then. An important step forward was taken with the writings of psychiatrist Eric Lindemann on the subject of grief. In Boston, in 1942, there was a terrible fire in a nightclub known as the "Coconut Grove." This fire involved enormous loss of life. In attendance were young college couples from two schools with a longstanding football rivalry. They were celebrating the annual contest between the two campuses on the night when fire broke out. It spread quickly through the dance floor, and four hundred and ninety-two lives were lost. Many were crushed in a stampede to escape through fire exits, exits which turned out to be locked.

Dr. Lindemann (1944) studied the response of these and other victims, and wrote the first paper to outline the grief syndrome as an important component of the aftermath of traumatic events. The syndrome includes marked sighing, lack of strength or energy, intense subjective distress, guilt, loss of warmth for others, possible feelings of hostility, preoccupation with death and the deceased, and sometimes taking on the appearance of traits of the deceased. These were important findings, but many years would pass before successful interventions would be developed to incorporate these findings in ways that brought relief to victims.

*Emergency Services Personnel.* In 1974, psychologist Jeffrey Mitchell had been observing a rapid turnover of nursing staff in a shock trauma center of a large general hospital in Baltimore. When he inquired about this matter, he was told that the nurses were leaving after several months because of the stress caused by the number of severe gunshot wounds to the head and other violent situations, which brought profoundly injured people to the center.

Was this a variant of the grief syndrome? Could anything now be done to assist these nurses and other emergency service providers encountering similar situations in their rescue work?

In seeking to answer these questions, Dr. Mitchell (1983) proposed the need for a series of systematic, comprehensive interventions, based on principles of crisis intervention. Over time, this approach has been developed by subsequent authors, and is now known as Critical Incident Stress Management (CISM; Everly & Mitchell, 1997).

Early CISM service delivery efforts focused on a group intervention known as Critical Incident Stress Debriefing (CISD; Mitchell, 1983; Mitchell & Everly, 1996). CISD is a group intervention approach in which relief personnel gather after the disaster or act of violence to review the facts, thoughts, emotions, PTSD symptoms, associated with each event as well as helpful strategies for coping with the psychological aftermath of these incidents.

The CISD approach was first used publicly during the crash of the Air Florida Flight 90 into the Fourteenth Street Bridge in Washington, D.C., in 1982. Its success in helping the onsite emergency services personnel with their personal reactions to this tragedy was quickly recognized, and has led to the development of over some 700 CISD quick-response teams worldwide.

As the general level of violence in society has increased in frequency and extent, new intervention needs have emerged. Many episodes of violence are single individual episodes that do not easily lend themselves to group intervention approaches. Other events, such as drive-by shootings of young children, impact not only emergency service providers but surviving family members as well. Over time, these emerging needs have led service providers to return to Mitchell's early concept of a multifactional approach (Mitchell, 1983), and to add additional services beyond CISD (Mitchell & Everly, 1996), such as consultations and referrals for counseling. Preliminary findings indicate the efficacy of this CISM approach for emergency services personnel and other populations (Everly & Mitchell, 1997).

*Health Care Providers.* During these same years, there was another group of victims whose needs were similarly being overlooked. Year after year, health care workers in emergency rooms, acute care units, delivery rooms, and psychiatric units were continually assaulted by those patients whom they sought to serve. Many victims tried denial, the passage of time, and informal support as coping strategies. However, many remained victims of untreated PTSD (Caldwell, 1992).

In September, 1989, I was asked to consult with the senior managers of a large state mental hospital. Both the management and the unions were concerned about health care employees who were being assaulted by psychiatrically ill persons. A recent spate of unacceptable incidents challenged the hospital to seek a way to address the issue.

While I knew about the effectiveness of the CISD approach, the needs of the hospital staff were varied and complex. While some episodes of violence did disrupt entire ward units that could benefit from the CISD approach, more common were episodes of single-event violence. Further complicating matters was the fact that many of the employee victims were single parents, and, when they went home with bruises on the heads, their children became understandably frightened and did not want their parents to return to work. Still other staff had been employees in the hospital for many years and had been assaulted several times intermittently throughout their employment periods. While some attempted to remain stoic, a recent assault resulting in painful memories of earlier patient assaults was the more common outcome. Assaults in the facility were a daily and costly fact of life. Something needed to be done.

It was clear to me that no one intervention, no matter how effective in its own right, could address the differing needs of the employee victims in this facility. These differing situations suggested the need for a CISM approach (Everly & Mitchell, 1997), and led to my developing the *Assaulted Staff Action Program* (ASAP; Flannery et al. 1991).

The ASAP program (Flannery 1995, 1997, 1998; Flannery et al., 1991; Flannery et al., 1995; Flannery et al., 1996) is a voluntary peer-help, system-wide, crisis intervention approach for health care staff who are assaulted by patients. ASAP was designed to include several different types of crisis interventions for the differing types of episodes of violence noted earlier. These include individual debriefings for each staff victim, a staff victims' support group, CISD for entire ward units, employee-victim family counseling, and a referral service to professional counselors trained in treating psychological trauma, when indicated.

Research studies (Flannery, Hanson, & Penk, 1994; Flannery et al., 1995; Flannery et al., 1996) suggest that ASAP is efficacious in providing needed support to employee victims in a cost-effective manner, and appears to prevent the onset of untreated PTSD. ASAP is also associated with sharp reductions in violence in some hospital facilities, where it has been fielded.

In this chapter we shall explore the ASAP program that has been designed to deal with the aftermath of the violence that we have examined at length. First, we shall outline the ASAP program, including its rationale, its structure, and its services. Then, we shall turn our attention to the empirical findings that document the helpfulness of the approach.

In this presentation I will focus on health care settings, but, again, ASAP is easily modifiable for other settings, such as those noted in the examples that begin each chapter and in the various settings that we have listed earlier. We now have sufficient ASAP technologies to address the needs of a variety of victims.

## THE ASSAULTED STAFF ACTION PROGRAM (ASAP)

### ASAP: Philosophy and Basic Assumptions

The ASAP program is predicated on several basic assumptions that are thought to lessen the psychological sequelae of assaults on employee victims and that enhance communities of compassion in the facilities where they are located. Central to this process is the concept of developing *Stress- Resistant Persons* (Flannery, 1990, 1994). These persons are able to develop and maintain reasonable mastery, caring attachments, and a meaningful purpose in life, skills that are helpful in coping adequately, and skills that are frequently disrupted by traumatic events as we have noted.

### *Stress-Resistant Persons*

Over the centuries physicians have noted that some men and women, when confronted with stressful life events, cope adaptively and emerge relatively intact from these events whereas others, faced with the same events are overwhelmed and become ill. ASAP has as its goal the instilling or restoring of these adaptive skills in victims so that victims do not become overwhelmed and ill.

While medicine and the behavioral sciences have focused understandable attention on illness and its treatment, less attention has been paid to the adaptive problem solvers who cope adequately and avoid frequent illness. In the 1950s, psychiatrist Lawrence Hinkle (Hinkle & Wolfe, 1958) studied working class men and women in the telephone company in New York City. In examining patterns of sick leave, he found that more people called in sick on Mondays and Fridays than on the other days of the week. When he spoke to those on sick leave, he found that many were attempting to cope with a number of stressful life situations. Dr. Hinkle and his colleagues also noted that some employees rarely called in sick, yet, when he contacted these healthy employees, they often had as many problems as those who were out on sick leave. However, unlike those who were ill, these healthy employees exercised reasonable control over their lives (and stressful life events), and they had adequate networks of caring attachments.

The 1970s saw a second major research project to study effective adult problem-solvers conducted by psychologists Salvatore Maddi and Suzanne Kobasa (Maddi & Kobasa, 1984). Their efforts were focused on the psychological factors that would ensure good health and functioning in the senior managers of large corporations and professional groups, such as lawyers.

They identified three important factors. The first was control, or reasonable mastery over daily personal and work responsibilities. The second was commitment to something of importance to them, and the third factor was to be able to respond to change as a challenge rather than as a burden. Persons with these factors were more effective managers and professionals, and had better health as measured by a variety of outcome measures.

Having worked in a psychiatric emergency service for several years where we would see some patients very frequently and others not at all, these two research projects stirred my curiosity, particularly the questions left unanswered by these first two projects. Were the findings of adequate coping skills true for the large middle class as well as the working class (Hinkle) and the upper middle class (Maddi)? Were these skills similar for both men and women or were there important gender differences? Were people born with these skills or could they be learned?

To address these matters, I designed and fielded a research project in the 1980s that assessed the coping skills of 1,200 adult men and women over a twelve-year period (Flannery, 1990, 1994). The subjects of this study were attending college classes in the evening at the end of their work day. Most worked full-time, had family responsibilities, and attended classes two to three evenings per week. They had to drive to the university in major rush-hour traffic, and often had snacks in class for energy. Their lives reflected many of the stressful life events faced by all of us at the end of the Twentieth Century.

Some were ill and missed classes. Others had nearly perfect attendance. This seemed like an ideal group for the study of effective coping with life stress.

From among this group, my colleagues and I identified those men and women who coped effectively with stressful life events so that they avoided, for the most part, the negative impact such events could have on health and general functioning. I refer to these men and women as *Stress-Resistant Persons*. Here is what we have learned.

Stress-resistant persons appear to use six strategies to cope successfully with stressful life events. These effective strategies result in better physical health, less anxiety and depression, sustained daily functioning, and a sense of well-being, and are listed in table 1.

# Table 1

## Stress-Resistant Persons:

1. Reasonable Mastery
2. Personal Commitment to Task
3. Wise Lifestyle Choices  - Few Dietary Stimulants
                                             - Aerobic Exercise
                                             - Relaxation Exercises
4. Social Support
5. Sense of Humor
6. Concern for Welfare of Others

1. *Reasonable Mastery.*  Our findings are similar to those of Drs. Hinkle, Maddi, Kobasa, and their colleagues.  Men and women who take personal control of their lives have better health.  They correctly identify the problem to be solved, gather information on possible solutions, develop strategies to address the matter at hand, choose a possible solution, and implement it, and then evaluate its effectiveness.  They also recognize that they are not able to solve some problems, and they do not waste unnecessary energy at these tasks.

2. *Personal Commitment to Task.*  Medicine and behavioral science have known for many years that individuals need a reason to live, a purpose in life that makes them want to invest their energy each day in the world around them.  This purpose may involve work, family, community, or artistic goals, and sustains these individuals, even when the going may be difficult.  Persons with goals have more energy, and are better able to cope with stressful life events of any type.

3. *Wise Lifestyle Choices.*  Stress-resistant persons know that we live in a fast-paced, computer-driven world of technology, but they have not forgotten that a sound body results in a sound mind.  Not surprisingly then, we found that effective problem solvers have found ways to reduce their  physiological states of high arousal and overdrive.  First, they reduce or eliminate the dietary stimulants of nicotine and caffeine.  These stimulants can turn on the body's emergency mobilization response, even when the person is not faced with a stressful situation, and stress-resistant persons avoid them.  Stress-resistant persons are also engaged in aerobic exercise at least three times a week over a seven day period.  These sessions last for twenty minutes or longer.  Such exercise is good for general health, and is the most effective way to reduce the body's physiological arousal due to stress.  Relaxation exercises for as little as ten minutes each day is the third wise lifestyle choice.  Formal systems of relaxation and meditation can be helpful in this regard as can sitting quietly, listening to soft music, praying, knitting, or doing crossword puzzles.

4. *Social Support.*  Caring attachments to others includes powerful physiological and psychological benefits.  On the physiological level, caring human contact may stabilize and strengthen heart rate, and stabilize and lower blood pressure.  It may

also enhance the capacity of the immune system to resist the onset of certain types of illnesses as well as stimulate endorphin circulation in the brain so that we feel better. On a psychological plane, attachments to others may provide us with needed emotional support, companionship, helpful information for problem solving, and tangible offers of money, political favors, or material goods. Stress-resistant persons intuitively understand these potential benefits and seek them out in their own lives. They are not socially isolated men and women.

5. *Humor.* Humor helps us to see the paradoxes in life over which one has no control, and laughing itself reduces the physiology of stress. Stress-resistant persons employ a sense of humor, if they have one. If not, they spend time with those who do.

6. *Concern for the Welfare of Others.* All of the great religions and ethical codes of the world espouse the basic responsibility of concern for the welfare of others: love one another. Even in an era that values personal entitlement and personal gain, our studies indicated that those motivated for the welfare of others enjoyed better health (Flannery, 1984).

Our research findings also enabled us to answer some of the questions that we posed earlier. The characteristics of stress-resistant persons are as accurate and helpful for the middle class as well as the other social classes. People do not appear to be born with these skills, but rather to learn them over time. Lastly, although men and women may express these characteristics in somewhat differing ways, there appear to be no inherent gender differences.

We also realized that stress-resistant persons used these six characteristics to ensure proper functioning in the three basic domains necessary for proper health and functioning; mastery, attachment, and meaning. They used the characteristics of reasonable mastery, wise lifestyle choices, and a sense of humor to ensure reasonable mastery. They utilized personal commitment to a task, social support, and concern for others to strengthen caring attachments, and they also employed commitment to a task, social support, and concern for others to develop and sustain a meaningful purpose in life.

Since earlier studies had shown us that teaching the skills of stress-resistant persons was a helpful component in the recovery of trauma victims (Flannery, Perry, & Harvey, 1993) and persons with serious mental illness, many of whom are also victims of traumatic violence (Starkey, Di Leone, & Flannery, 1995), fostering the characteristics of stress-resistant persons was selected as a clinical goal for all ASAP crisis interventions.

*Basic Assumptions*

In addition to this basic philosophy of stress-resistance, the ASAP program is guided by six basic assumptions. We believe that:

1. Staff members may experience a traumatic crisis as a result of patient assaults.
2. Such violence does not "come with the turf."
3. Employee victims are worthy of compassionate care.
4. The episode of violence is not the deliberate fault of the employee. The employee may have made technical errors that will require further training, but these errors are different from seeking to inflict harm on the patient with deliberate intent. (These latter cases of true criminal assault are dealt with according to standard state legal procedures.)
5. Employee victims are better able to speak about the event with peers who are at the same risk for being assaulted.
6. Talking about the event will lead to less human suffering and more effective coping in the short-term, and will avoid long-lasting disruptions, including untreated PTSD.

**ASAP: Structure**

ASAP programs and their teams vary in size and composition depending on the size of the facility, the frequency of assaults, and the number of patient-care sites that are included for ASAP services. We shall focus on the basic model that has been developed for state mental hospitals and that is outlined in table 2. This model is suitable for facilities with 150 to 400 beds, and with up to 400 direct care staff. An ASAP team for a facility of this size would require fifteen volunteer ASAP staff members and the hospital's switchboard operators.

Eleven of these ASAP volunteers constitute the first-line responders. Drawn from all disciplines including clinicians, managers, and mental health workers, the first line responders provide the ASAP response and crisis intervention for each individual

# Table 2

## ASAP Structure for Mental Hospital Setting:

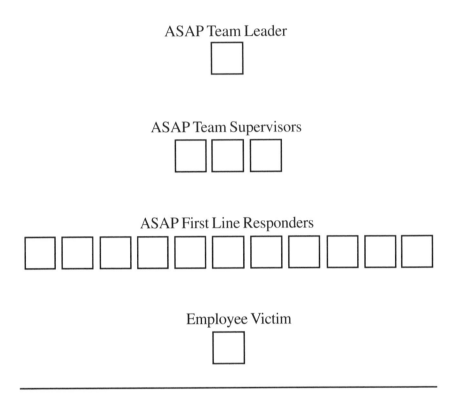

ASAP Team Leader

ASAP Team Supervisors

ASAP First Line Responders

Employee Victim

episode of assault. When an assault occurs, the charge nurse on the unit is required to call in the assault to the hospital switchboard. The operator summons the ASAP team member on call by page-beeper to respond to the particular episode of assault. The ASAP responder arrives onsite within fifteen minutes and offers the employee victim ASAP services. If the victim accepts, the individual crisis intervention is completed as described below. When the responder has finished, the same responder offers to call or visit the employee victim in three days, and, again, in ten days. In particularly disruptive assaults, the employee victims may also be immediately referred to the ASAP staff victims' group. In addition, first responders assess any needs for CISD for entire units and for possible employee-victim family counseling. These needs are communicated to the team leader. Every effort is made to ensure continuity of care.

First responders are on-call for twenty-four-hour periods on weekday rotations, and are on-call one weekend of every three months. In addition to individual crisis interventions, first responders attend a weekly one-hour ASAP team meeting during the weeks that they are on-call and a monthly in-service training on various aspects of PTSD and general team functioning. First responders spend an average of three hours per week on ASAP-related tasks, and, as a group, spend a total of about seventy-two hours per month. One page-beeper is rotated daily.

Three additional volunteers comprise the ASAP supervisors, who are also on-call by a second page-beeper. ASAP supervisors do not provide traditional clinical or administrative supervision. In ASAP they provide second opinions to first line responders, when needed; perform individual crisis interventions in cases of multiple assaults at the same time; and conduct CISD ward debriefings for entire patient-care units. The supervisors attend all weekly team meetings as well as the monthly in-service programs. ASAP supervisors are often senior nurse supervisors or senior staff development personnel. This allows for informal outreach to victims who have both accepted and declined ASAP services, and for the indirect assessment of needs for further staff training in patient-care issues related to violence. Supervisors rotate coverage weekly, and spend about ten hours each week on ASAP tasks for a supervisory total of about forty hours per month. A second page-beeper is rotated weekly.

The final volunteer is the ASAP team leader who is charged with administering the program and monitoring its overall quality. The team leader co-chairs a weekly staff victims' support group, and co-leads CISD unit debriefings as they are needed. Team leaders are responsible for on-call rotation coverages, for meeting weekly with the hospital switchboard operators, for conducting weekly ASAP team meetings to review all cases, for training new team members, for providing monthly in-service training, and for keeping track of the paper work and requisite data collection needed to ensure proper team functioning.

The team leader has a special role in monitoring the ASAP team members for vicarious traumatization which can arise from exposure to the impact of violent events in the course of conducting debriefings (McCann & Pearlman, 1990), and for being the individual crisis debriefer when ASAP team members are assaulted themselves or encounter other types of traumatic events. One ASAP team member's daughter, age eight, died from sudden cardiac arrest at school, while her mother was at work. Another team member had his two best friends murdered in their home by a drug-addicted intruder. Others have sustained injuries from patient assaults (bruises, scaldings) in their non-ASAP, hospital-related duties. Being an ASAP team member does not eliminate the possibility of being a victim of violence, and the ASAP team leader is responsible for taking care of his or her own. The ASAP director spends about fifteen hours a week on the program for a monthly total of sixty hours.

The hospital's switchboard operators, while not formal members of the ASAP program, are an integral component of the ASAP service delivery system. They are debriefed regularly by the team leader, as we have noted; are included in all ASAP in-service trainings; and are present at all ASAP social gatherings.

## ASAP: Services

With this basic structure in place, the ASAP team is then ready to provide the basic services listed in table 3. ASAP services emphasize the principles in military medicine of proximity, immediacy, and expectancy (Grinker & Spiegel, 1945). The employee victim is treated near the site of the assault, as quickly as possible, and with the expectation of the employee's returning to work.

*Individual Crisis Intervention.* When assault occurs and the charge nurse summons the ASAP team member on-call, the first line responder goes directly onsite, checks to be sure that safety and any needed medical issues have been addressed, and then reconstructs the facts of the assault. When these tasks are completed, the first responder introduces himself or herself to the employee victim, offers the ASAP intervention, and assures the employee victim of complete confidentiality, unless the employee victim reports a crime.

If the employee victim accepts the service, the first responder begins by monitoring the victim for the presence of any symptoms associated with psychological trauma as well as any disruptions in

# Table 3

## ASAP Services:

---

1. Individual Crisis Interventions
2. CISD for Patient-Care Sites
3. Staff Victims' Support Group
4. Employee Victim Family Counseling
5. Professional Referrals

---

the domains of mastery, attachment, and meaning. Staff victims are encouraged to talk freely about the violent act and any negative thoughts or feelings that it may have generated. The ASAP team member listens quietly, and helps the victim reconstruct what has taken place. Should the first responder encounter an employee victim with flashbacks from previous acts of violence for which the current assault has served as a symbolic reminder, the responder calms the employee, states the fact of the victim's experience of intrusive memories to the victim, reassures the victim that the victim is on the ward unit, and assists in integrating the intrusive memories.

Next, the first responder attempts to develop a plan with the active input of the employee victim to return the employee to some level of pre-incident functioning that seems suitable. For example, in the area of mastery, employee victims are asked if they feel that they are able to remain on the unit; whether they would like time off the unit for record-keeping tasks; whether they would like to speak to the offending patient, when safety has been restored; and similar suggestions to restore some initial sense of control for the victim. The first responder also assesses the resources available for caring attachments networks. The ASAP member and program is one such network of attachments, and possibilities with colleagues, supervisors, family, and friends are explored. The team member then tries to help the victim make some initial sense of what happened. Perhaps the patient was not on medication, or had a difficult time at the patient's day program. ASAP team members are especially alert for victim self-blaming and victim-blaming by others, and these are dealt with directly, if they are present.

The staff victim is notified that the same team member will call in three days, and again in ten days. The victim is encouraged to remain in contact, and is given a card with the ASAP team members name and hospital phone extension, should the staff member want to call at any time. All employee victims, including those who decline ASAP, are given written information in handout format on psychological trauma, practical suggestions for coping, help for families, and the names and extensions of all ASAP team members. (See figure 18.)

If an assault occurs when the ASAP team member is not onsite, the first responder calls the unit and assesses the situation with the charge nurse and the employee victim. If all are in agreement that the debriefing needs to be done immediately, the ASAP team member returns to the hospital and conducts the crisis intervention. If it is deemed not urgent, the same team member makes arrangements to meet the staff victim the next day. Team members responding during off-duty hours may be given compensatory time off within the next thirty days. ASAP team members receive no financial compensation.

On rare occasions, the employee victim's injuries from the patient assault may require attention at an emergency room or other medical facility. Subject to administrative approval and staffing at the time, ASAP team members may accompany the employee victim to the medical facility and complete the ASAP debriefing there. This provides important support to a colleague, and demonstrates ASAP's commitment to the hospital community. The ASAP supervisor covers the hospital's ASAP needs, while the ASAP first responder is offsite. (A few ASAP facilities have adopted a written policy for this infrequent event.)

Finally, when the first line responder is debriefing an employee victim, the ASAP team member's colleagues on the team member's patient-care site cover for the team member during the hour that he or she is off of the unit.

If an employee victim declines the ASAP service, he or she is given a card with the first responder's name and hospital phone extension, in case the victim has a change of mind.

*CISD for Patient-Care Sites.* From time to time, particularly violent events may occur on patient-care sites. For example, on one acute admissions unit a patient went into a state of rage after a family visit. He assaulted several staff, put one nurse on a window sill and threatened to push her to her death several stories below, hurled furniture indiscriminately around the unit, before being finally subdued by a phalanx of male attendants. Staff were injured, patient witnesses to this event were frightened, and the managers temporarily felt out of control. There were sharp increases in fear, anger, and various forms of behavioral disorganization.

In circumstances such as these, the ASAP program utilizes a second crisis intervention procedure, CISD (Mitchell & Everly, 1996). This group process involves a review of the actual facts of the event; an update on the health status of the victims; and a focus on the thoughts, feelings, and symptoms that victims or witnesses may be experiencing. This is followed by a brief discussion of psychological trauma and its impact as well as suggestions for coping more adaptively in the coming days. It is a helpful approach because its structure prevents the discussion of powerful emotions within a structured, containing format. [See Mitchell and Everly (1996) for a detailed presentation on how to conduct CISD debriefings.]

ASAP CISD interventions are conducted by the ASAP team leader and one or more of the ASAP team supervisors. Typically, this includes three separate CISD interventions. The first is held for the unit managers on the assumption that mitigating the impact of the event here first will result in the managers' being of assistance to the rest of the unit's staff and patients in need. In addition to this debriefing, the goals of the management team for resolving the clinical aftermath of the event are sought. Questions such as whether the violent patient is to remain on the ward, whether other patients can request a transfer, how coverage for the employee victims on leave will be covered are addressed in some detail, so that this information is available in subsequent ASAP CISD interventions for the unit.

A second CISD is then conducted for the patient-care site staff. Coverage is arranged so that the staff can be released for this meeting. The CISD proceeds with special attention focused on their injured colleagues, and the staff's reactions to the violence. At the end of the process, the goals and decisions of the senior managers are discussed. The managers usually do not sit in on this debriefing in order that the staff may freely express their fears and anger, including that the management failed to protect them.

A third debriefing is held for the entire ward community with management, staff, and patients present. The goal of this third CISD intervention is to address the needs of the patient community. Our experience has been that it is difficult for persons with impaired functioning, including many who have also been victims of violence at other times in their lives, to process violent episodes on their own unit, where issues of safety are a reasonable concern. Addressing the management and staff needs first frees these employees to be supportive of patients during this third debriefing. Depending on the level of disorganization in the patient community, CISD interventions are shortened and/or repeated on several occasions, until some sense of unit order and calm is restored. Debriefings can be held for all three shifts, if the circumstances of the event warrant this.

The ASAP program offers to meet with each and all of the three groups for further CISD debriefings or individual consultations, makes available written information on trauma and coping, and generally monitors the situation.

*Staff Victims' Support Group.* Some victims need additional ongoing, short-term support, and ASAP provides this through a staff victims' support group. Co-lead by the ASAP team leader and one ASAP supervisor, the group focuses on the issues of restoring mastery, attachment, and meaning as well as developing active strategies to cope with any remaining symptomatology. Staff victims for whom the current patient assault has led to intrusive memories of previous assaults or other types of traumatic events are referred in time for private treatment, if it is needed.

To facilitate attendance at the staff victims' group, employee victims are given staff release time to attend, and are paid their hourly wage for attendance at group sessions during off-shifts. The group is held midafternoon to make it readily available to employees on two of the hospital's three shifts.

*Employee Victim Family Counseling.* Occasionally, an employee assault is particularly distressing to the employee's family members. They may experience acute distress, and not want the employee to return to work. This is especially true of single-parent employees where the children may fear becoming orphans, if the parent is fatally injured at work. The active resistance of the children creates a difficult situation for the parent, who may need to return to work for needed income.

In circumstances such as these, ASAP offers family counseling services for its employee family members. These sessions can occur at the employee's home or at the hospital, and focus on restoring mastery, attachment, and meaning within the family unit. Each family member is given the opportunity to discuss fears, potential acts of further violence are put in perspective, and the family members are given practical suggestions on how to cope and restore normal family functioning. Again, this ASAP service may be repeated as often as needed, but our experience suggests that it is needed very infrequently, and then only once per assaultive episode.

*Professional Referrals.* When traumatic events at the hospital have served as symbolic reminders of previous episodes of non-work related violence, the ASAP program provides professional referrals to counselors who are trained in addressing the psychological aftermath of traumatic events. Each ASAP team leader has a list of trauma intervention programs and specific trauma therapists in their own geographical area.

For example, one common outcome is for an episode of patient assault to stir memories of earlier incidents of child battering or spousal battering. After the individual crisis debriefing, these employee victims are referred to the Staff Victims' Support Group, and, at times, individual sessions with the ASAP team leader. These meetings are intended to provide support to the employee, to address any sense of shame that may be experienced by the employee, and to provide a gentle transition to the private counselor or specialized trauma program.

All ASAP interventions are fully confidential, unless the employee victim reports a crime. (In these cases, all employees are governed by state regulations to formally report such violations.) ASAP records do not become part of any medical record, any personnel record, nor any employee performance review appraisal. All ASAP records are kept within the ASAP program in a locked cabinet that belongs to the team leader. Any employee wishing his or her ASAP report forwarded to a third party, such as the family physician or Industrial Accident Claims Board, meets with the team leader, reviews the ASAP records with the ASAP team leader, and signs an ASAP release of information form. The employee victim's records are then forwarded as requested. (See figure 19.) Informed consent is obtained from all employees, and data are collected on all episodes of assault. The team leader codes this data, which is collected only in the aggregate. The data is used only for the general purposes of quality management and to increase our understanding of violence and how to address it.

Finally, with the exception of private individual counseling sessions by trauma specialists, all ASAP services are free employee benefits, and staff are encouraged by both management and unions to avail themselves of these services.

## VIOLENCE IN HEALTH CARE SETTINGS: PATIENT ASSAULTS

### Characteristics of Assaultive Psychiatric Patients.

Information about the characteristics of assaultive patients in health care settings that we are about to review, and the early warning signs of impending loss of control that we shall summarize shortly are important to employees in decreasing the risk of their being victims, and to ASAP team members who can utilize this information to help employee victims reconstruct the facts of any given episode of violence to help them make meaningful sense of what has happened. They are noted here briefly to augment our earlier general discussion of aggression with violence specific to the health care settings in which ASAP has been fielded.

While employees in health care settings may be victims of homicides, rapes, and robberies (American Psychiatric Association, 1992), health care providers have been primarily at-risk from violence due to patient assaults. There is an extensive published literature spanning twenty-five years that yields clear and consistent findings in terms of the types of assault, the characteristics of the assailants, and the environments in which these aggressive outbursts may occur. [The interested reader is referred to reviews of this literature by Blair (1991), Davis (1991), and Flannery, Hanson, and Penk (1994)].

Assaults by psychiatric patients are grouped in four classes of violence: physical assault, sexual assault, nonverbal intimidation, and verbal threat. Any of these acts of aggression, including verbal threat, may result in psychological trauma (Flannery, Hanson, & Penk, 1995).

1.  *Physical Assaults* are defined as any acts of unwanted physical contact with intent to harm. Included here are events such as biting; kicking; slapping; punching; spitting; throwing of objects directly at staff such as knives, physical objects, or scalding liquids.

2.  *Sexual Assaults* are any acts of unwanted sexual contact. These include rape, attempted rape, fondling, or exposing one's self.

3.  *Nonverbal Intimidation* refers to any behaviors or acts that are meant to frighten or intimidate staff. Kicking the door of the nurses' station; throwing objects, such as furniture in the environment; rageful or menacing leering or staring; stalking of staff; destruction of staff property; and the throwing of potentially harmful objects in the general direction of, but not at, staff are examples of nonverbal intimidation.

4.  *Verbal Threats* are verbal statements meant to frighten or intimidate staff. Threats to kill staff or staff family members, threats to destroy staff property, threats to report false charges about staff, racial epithets, and other discriminatory or derogatory statements are illustrations of common types of verbal threats.

Considerable research attention has been directed toward the characteristics of the patients who commit these acts of violence. (Blair, 1991; Davis, 1991; Flannery et al.,1994), and the findings are generally uniform.

Younger male patients who have a diagnosis of psychosis with active and impaired thinking or some neurological abnormality have been found to be more prone to assaultive behavior. In addition, these patients have histories of violence toward others, and past and/or current histories of substance abuse, as is shown in table 4. Since the assessment of histories of personal victimization is a recent area of inquiry, these studies have not consistently evaluated these patients for their own untreated PTSD. Younger male patients who are actively psychotic, who are hearing persecutory voices, and who are currently using substances abusively, pose the greatest single threat.

The employees most at risk for these assaults are younger male mental health workers with less formal education, training, and experience, and nurses who are assaulted during restraint and seclusion procedures.  These assaults may be either unprovoked as staff perform their duties or sustained when patients are restrained. Most assaults occur during meal times, and  bruises with swelling are the most common form of injury.

The research findings have also indicated common precipitants to these aggressive outbursts and characteristics of the patient-care sites that contribute to increased risk for violence, and these have also been summarized in table 4.

Of the known precipitants, the denial of services and patient requests is the most common stimulus for angry outbursts.  Losing ground or weekend privileges, being required to forgo family or community visits may also result in violence.  Similarly, sensory overload may lead to cognitive disorganization.  Most assaults occur during mealtimes, and these are the periods when unit activity is most intense.  In addition to meals, there are staff shift changes, patients going to day programs, family and guests visiting, and the like.  For fragile brain chemistry, events such as these may prove psychologically and neurologically overwhelming, and may result in violent behaviors.

Restraint procedures are a third common precursor to violence.  Staff activity to surround and contain an out-of-control patient may further frighten the patient, who correctly perceives himself or herself to be boxed in.  In addition, since many of these patients have histories of personal victimization, the restraint and seclusion procedures themselves may serve as symbolic reminders of past painful events, and the patient may experience additional hypervigilance, extreme fright, and intrusive memories from the procedure itself.  For example, if a female patient has been the victim of sexual abuse by a male family member, being surrounded by male staff who hold the female patient against her will, carry her to a seclusion room, strap her down with her legs spread apart, and then inject her with medicine in the buttocks can itself be fully re-traumatizing biologically and psychologically.  Rage may ensue.

The research literature has also revealed consistent patient-care site characteristics that may increase the risk of violent outbursts.  Patient-care sites that have weak administrative leadership

# Table 4

## Risk Factors for Patient Assaults:

---

*Patient* - Young Male
- Diagnosis of Psychosis or Neurological Abnormalities
- History of Violence Toward Others
- History of Substance Abuse


*Precipitants*      - Denial of Service
- Sensory Overload
- Restraint Procedures


*Patient-Care Sites*       - Weak Administrative Leadership
- Unclear Staff Roles and Functions
- Unstructured Unit Activities
- Inadequate Staffing
- Inadequate Training
- Culture of Toughness

---

or a lax milieu appear to have more unit violence (Flannery, Hanson, Penk, & Flannery, 1996). Weak leadership often results in unclear staff roles and functions. A milieu of unstructured unit activities complicated by inadequate staffing or inadequate staff training further increases the likelihood of violence.

In many psychiatric settings, a culture of toughness (Morrison, 1990) is also present. In these patient-care settings, the staff assumes that aggressive patient behavior is due to impulsivity, a medical problem that is viewed as out of the patient's control. The obvious corollary to this belief is a second assumption that the patient must be controlled. This leads to the use of medication, time outs (involuntary periods of isolation somewhere on the unit), restraints, and seclusion. Talking matters over with the patient or utilizing other alternatives to restraint and seclusion are minimized. Policing and control become dominant, and the staff have to be "tough" to communicate to the patient community the importance of control and order. This culture of toughness itself may engender further patient violence.

It is important to note that the studies cited here have been conducted primarily with psychiatric inpatients. During recent years there has been a national movement toward privatization of psychiatric health care and the placement of patients in the community. Little is known of the nature of assaults on staff by psychiatric patients in community settings. One study (Flannery, Hanson, Penk, & Flannery, 1994b) noted that younger female staff were at increased risk for sexual assaults by older male patients, but much experimental inquiry remains to be undertaken in this area.

**Warning Signs of Impending Loss of Control**

Since there is no known way to predict violence with one hundred percent accuracy, health care providers have learned to monitor patients for the possible warning signs of potential loss of control, and these are listed in table 5. There are three areas of concern: known medical disorders, appearances, and behaviors.

As we saw in chapter one, certain types of medical disorders may be associated with aggressive behaviors. Psychiatric health care settings have at least four of these disorders present. These include serious mental illness, Organic Personality Syndromes, substance abuse, and probably untreated PTSD. As we have seen, these disorders may be risk factors for violence.

Changes in appearance constitute the second area of warning signs. Disorganization in physical dress or appearance may include being disheveled, unshaven, and generally ill-kempt. Tense facial expressions may result from attempts to contain anger. Glazed eyes are frequently associated with substance abuse that may result in cortical disinhibition. The use of dark glasses on cloudy days or indoors may indicate paranoia or substance abuse. Similarly, long-sleeve shirts in hot weather may indicate drug abuse by needle injection.

Angry behaviors form the third grouping of warning signs. These include the behavior signs of severe agitation like pacing, pounding, and staring, as well as verbally hostile and argumentative statements. Suggestions of substance abuse such as uncoordinated movement, slurred speech, or alcohol on the person's breath are signs of possible loss of control. Likewise, threats of weapons and verbal threats to harm specific persons should be seen as statements from a person in tenuous control at best.

# Table 5

## Warning Signs of Loss of Control:

1. *Medical Disorders Associated with Aggressive Outbursts*
2. *Appearance*
    - Disorganized in Physical Dress or Appearance
    - Tense Facial Expressions
    - Glazed Eyes
    - Inappropriate Use of Dark Glasses
    - Long Sleeves in Hot Weather
3. *Behavior*
    - Behavioral Signs of Severe Agitation
    - Verbally Hostile and Argumentative
    - Suggestions of Substance Abuse
    - Verbal Threats to Specific Persons
    - Threat of Weapons

A generally helpful rule of thumb is this: the greater the number of warning signs that are present, the greater the likelihood that violence may erupt.

### Violence in Other Settings

Just as this information about patient assaults can be helpful to future ASAP team members in health care settings, other groups of persons can begin to study the violence in their environments. Information can be gathered on the types of crime and violence that are present, on the characteristics, or profiles the persons involved in these acts, and on the properties inherent in these environments that may be adding additional risk to the situation.

For example, in many schools there are unacceptably high levels of student-to-student violence and student-to-teacher violence. The published literature (Flannery, 1995) suggests that rape, robbery, and assaults are the most frequent crimes. Surveys in a school district of aggressive incidents could yield important information on the students most likely to commit these acts and the type of school environments that they are most likely to target.

As with the health care data, such information can lead to

environments that are more safe, and that provide needed information for the members of ASAP teams fielded in these sites on how to help victims make sense of what has happened.

## VIOLENCE IN HEALTH CARE SETTINGS: THE ASAP RESPONSE

**The Assaulted Staff Action Program in Health Care Settings.**
    To deal with the ongoing issue of helping victims of patient assault cope with the psychological aftermath of such events, the ASAP program is now fielded in ten sites in Massachusetts Department of Mental Health (DMH) facilities and DMH contracted provider agencies. These settings include state psychiatric hospitals, state community mental health centers, state homeless shelter programs, and provider community residential and day services programs.
    Over 150 ASAP team members have volunteered over 220,000 hours of service to these various facilities as they have provided ASAP services to 2,000 employees, who are, in turn, responsible for 3,000 patients. Two additional ASAP teams are about to come on-line, and facilities in two other states are considering fielding ASAP teams. No ASAP team member has ever requested his or her earned comp time.
    The ASAP program has acted as a consultant to the state's Department of Corrections as it designed a debriefing model for its prison facilities statewide. ASAP was chosen as one of ten finalists in 1996 for the American Psychiatric Association's Gold Medal Award, and has been cited in the recent guidelines for preventing violence in health care and social service agencies that have been issued by the Occupational Safety and Health Administration (OSHA, 1996).
    The ASAP program has had an important impact in three areas: clinical services, declines in frequency of violence, and dollar-cost savings. These findings are based on a series of research reports (Flannery et al., 1995; Flannery et al., 1996), which are included in chapter six for the interested reader, and which are summarized here briefly.

    *Clinical Services.* The ASAP crisis intervention procedures have provided needed support to employee victims, who most frequently experienced disrupted senses of reasonable mastery and meaningful sense of why these violent events have happened. These employee victims also frequently experienced the symptoms of hypervigilance, sleep disturbance, and intrusive memories. For most employee victims who accepted ASAP services, these disruptions and symptoms had passed within ten days. However, a full nine percent of these employee victims continued to report disruptions and symptoms for a period of months after the assault, a finding similar for reported data in other health care settings (Caldwell, 1992).

*Declines in Assault.* An unanticipated outcome in the original ASAP program was a sixty-three percent decline in the number of assaults over the two year period before that facility was closed. My original understanding of this serendipitous finding was that it was an artifact of the hospital's being closed. However, when ASAP was subsequently fielded in three different state mental hospitals, there was a similar forty percent decrease in the assault rate in *each* of these three facilities.(Flannery, Hanson, Penk, Goldfinger, Pastva, & Navon, 1998).

*Dollar-Cost Savings.* ASAP programs pay for themselves. Our studies have indicated that facilities with ASAP programs have less staff turnover due to assault-related issues. Fewer assaults result in fewer medical injuries, less sick leave utilization, less Industrial Accident Claims, less medical and legal expense, and sustained productivity.

In addition to these dollar-cost savings, ASAP programs provide a strong message of support to the workforce from management and the unions. This increases morale, and a sense of responsibility and concern for one another. In this way ASAP creates communities of compassion, a situation in which all parties involved benefit.

*How Does ASAP Work?* The answer to this question remains unknown at the time, and there are several ongoing research projects to assist in answering this question more fully.

In the interim, several possible explanations have been advanced. The various ASAP services appear to function in a manner similar to other crisis intervention procedures for victims of traumatic violence (Flannery, 1992, 1994). Early interventions that emphasize restoring mastery, attachment and meaning, that emphasize an assessment and monitoring of any of the symptoms associated with psychological trauma and untreated PTSD, and that discuss the event and its aftermath early on appear to contribute, in part, to a successful resolution of these matters for most employee victims. ASAP interventions focus on the here-and-now, and support the active involvement of the victim in planning and participating in the victim's recovery process, approaches known to assist victims of violence in their recoveries.

The declines in the frequency of violence are more difficult to explain. Several possible ASAP factors may be at work. First, an ASAP program supports its employees. It may be that, as they are supported, they become less tense. As the staff become less tense, the patients may become less tense, and, thus, the probability of assault decreases. ASAP permits the staff other responses to violence than that of imposing the control often associated with a ward culture of toughness (Morrison, 1989). It may be that ASAP interventions lead staff to pay more attention to the early warning signs that were noted in table 4, and to utilize alternatives to restraint and seclusion, so that potential violence is de-escalated before it reaches the level of loss of control and assault. This view is similar to fixing the broken window theory in policing (Kelling & Coles, 1996), which states that correcting the first signs of trouble early on avoids more severe violence later.

ASAP may also be at work in reducing the avoidance responses to patients by staff who have had untreated PTSD from earlier episodes of assault by patients, when there was no ASAP intervention program. These ASAP interventions may free some employees from the use of avoidance symptoms, and result in the delivery of better care by employees who are no longer fearful of the patients. It may also be that ASAP in some manner transforms the work environment from a culture of toughness to one of mutual support. The arrival onsite of an ASAP team member after each episode of violence is a strong nonverbal message that violence does not come with the turf.

Some combination of these factors, or those yet to be discovered, may account for part of the beneficial outcomes that occur when an ASAP program is fielded. However, it is unlikely that ASAP by itself is the sole factor. In those facilities where violence has declined after an ASAP program has been implemented, a number of other services to address for assaultive behaviors were already present. These included patient-at-risk conferences; medication, behavioral, and forensic consultations; standardized training in nonviolent self-defense and restraint and seclusion procedures as well as ongoing staff development programs. While these services did not reduce the level of violence in and of themselves before ASAP teams were fielded, it is likely that these services in conjunction with the ASAP program resulted in these beneficial outcomes. Further research is needed, particularly in community settings, where these clinical support services may not be routinely available

This completes our review of the essentials of an ASAP program. We have studied the rationale and conceptual framework of ASAP programs as well as their structures and services. ASAP programs exist to address the psychological aftermath of violence in health care settings and ASAP's exciting and beneficial outcomes, which are based on sound empirical research, suggest that an ASAP program is more beneficial to victims and their organization than some of the less formal approaches that we noted earlier. With today's technologies, there in no need for Ellen to be fearful of patients when she returns to work, nor for Henry, the subway motorman, to be faced with recurring flashbacks of the young girl in the fuchsia jacket, who jumped to her death in front of his train.

One of the great strengths of the ASAP approach is the flexibility of its design. ASAP programs can be adapted and modified for different types of environments where violence may be occurring once the basic steps in fielding a team are understood.

In the next chapter, we will examine those basic guidelines for building an ASAP team. For consistency in presentation, we shall use health care settings for purposes of illustration. However, readers in other settings where assaults or other types of violent acts may be occurring are again encouraged to design an ASAP program from the guidelines for their own setting.

With our general knowledge of violence, and our basic discussion of the ASAP program, let us now turn our attention to fielding a team.

# PART 2

## THE ASSAULTED STAFF ACTION PROGRAM (ASAP): PRACTICE

# Chapter

# 3

## ASAP: FIELDING THE TEAM

*Rage, rage against the dying of the light.*
- Dylan Thomas

*What wisdom can you find that is greater than kindness?*
- Jean Jacques Rousseau

Kill the body and the head will fall.

Angel lay on his bunk and thought about Mohammed Ali's fighting strategy. Hit repeatedly at the body of your opponent until he lowers his arms from his face to protect his body, then move to the head for the kill.

Angel ruminated on the strategy as he planned his revenge. No one cracked the wrist of a brother.

"Swing harder, keep your eye on your opponent. Watch his moves." The suggestions came from Jason Roberts, Little League coach and sheriff's county correction officer. For fifteen years, he had volunteered his weekends so that inner city youth would have a decent chance in life and not end up as prison inmates.

It had been a stressful week at the prison with several gang fights taking place in the maximum security cell block to which he was assigned. In breaking up one of these fights among two rival gangs, he had to pin one inmate against the wall. In this process, the inmate had slipped, and had accidentally cracked his wrist.

"Watch his movements. Keep your eyes on the ball."

The sun burned through the early morning fog on this humid summer's day, as Jason drove his pick-up truck to work. By 7:00 A.M., he was manning his cellblock for the day. After the inmates' breakfast, he was assigned to take gang leader, Angel Rose, to the infirmary. Angel, who was in for murder one, complained of stomach pains.

As Angel and Jason slowly walked the isolated corridor from the cellblock to the prison infirmary, Angel suddenly began punching Jason in the stomach. After several of Angel's repeated thrusts, Jason reached down reflexively to cover his chest and abdomen. Angel sprang at his head with a contraband razor blade, and slashed his face and throat again and again, until additional officers arrived and subdued him.

Jason lay bleeding on the concrete floor waiting for the medics to arrive. To keep himself going, he kept repeating to himself that dead men don't bleed.

Eighty-nine stitches were needed to staunch the flow of blood. One of Jason's retina was torn, and facial scarring would be permanent.

"Keep your eye on your opponent. Watch his moves."

Kill the body and the head will fall.

Night followed day.


Here is a third victim treated mercilessly at the hands of an assailant. What will be the response of the prison authorities to their wounded colleague? Like the health care agency and the transit authority in the two earlier examples that we have encountered, how will the organization respond to the psychological needs of their employee victim? Will Jason be left to his own resources for support, or will his peers support him in this crisis?

As we have seen, Jason needn't be left on his own. An ASAP program with a working knowledge of violence, psychological trauma, and crisis intervention procedures can be of important assistance to victims like Jason.

In this chapter, we examine in detail the mechanics of designing, training, and fielding an ASAP team for the needs of a variety of facilities. There are five basic steps in the process, which include 1.) obtaining administrative support, 2.) designing the team, 3.) selecting its members, 4.) training those members, and 5.) fielding the team within the facility.

For each step, the basic issues and possible solutions are outlined. Specific procedures that require corresponding specific forms are presented as accompanying, numbered figures. Since some issues are presented repeatedly in more than one of the five steps, figures are interspersed as needed, but all necessary forms will be found within this chapter. General comments on training are included here as step four. However, since training is a key component in the quality of all ASAP services that are rendered, training procedures and ASAP standards of performance and clinical practice guidelines are presented in detail in the next chapter. The service delivery report forms will be found there, again as numbered figures.

As we did in the last chapter, we will again use the state hospital as a basic design model. The Urban Hospital referred to in this chapter is fictitious; the issues and the forms are not.

This chapter contains a good deal of information that will need to be thought through for specific facility or environmental needs. We have found it helpful to do this in small manageable steps. In general, we allow ourselves at least one month to complete each step.

Finally, this chapter will be somewhat like completing your tax forms, but it is the best way to provide a comprehensive overview on how to field a team that is solidly grounded in ASAP policies and procedures. Since no ASAP program is successful without administrative support, we begin our inquiry there.

### 1. ADMINISTRATIVE SUPPORT

Administrative matters include management and union commitment to the ASAP program, legal matters, and financial costs.

### Management/ Union Commitment

*Management.* An ASAP program will not operate effectively without the full support of both management and unions. This implies a true understanding of victim need, knowledge of how ASAP functions, and a firm commitment to supporting both its being fielded and its ongoing delivery of services.

Managers begin by selecting some member of the

organization to head-up the task force needed to field a team. This choice can be a manager for this time-limited task, or, more ideally, the person who will ultimately be the team leader. All levels of management are told of the program, and are then asked for their input as to the system's needs for post-incident response to victims. The leader will later incorporate these suggestions, when the actual team is designed.

Managers need to agree to accept the confidentiality of ASAP records (see Legal Matters below), and to support both the delivery of ASAP services as well as the data collection process to monitor its quality.

In time, the ASAP program will have further unique needs for administrative support. For example, it is helpful if management encourages each discipline and each worksite to contribute some volunteers to the ASAP program. This facilitates a truly representative peer-help community, and, at the same time, is a strong message from the leadership about the importance of the program about to be fielded. This support in a state hospital system should include the chief operating officer, the medical director, the director of nursing, the patient-care unit chiefs, and the chiefs of each discipline.

Similarly, all incidents of assault are usually required to be reviewed by hospital policy, if not government regulations. This is understandable and needed to prevent further unnecessary injury. The ASAP program has learned over the years that, if the incident review and the ASAP debriefing are paired in time, many victims feel re-victimized when called upon to explain what happened. A more effective system appears to be assuring that everyone is safe, providing the ASAP debriefing, and, then, at a second point in time reviewing the case. For immediate safety reasons, the incident may well need to be reviewed within a few hours, and this should be done. However, if it is possible, it is better if the debriefing and the review are separated in time.

It is also common for assaults to be under reported (Lion, Snyder, & Merrill, 1981). Unit leadership does not want violence to reflect badly on the unit. Employees accept aggression as part of the job. A given act doesn't seem that serious. For these and other reasons, the management needs to mandate the reporting of assaults to the ASAP program (figure 7 ). Such hospital policy ensures accuracy and relieves each unit of any possible stigma associated with aggressive outbursts by patients. The ASAP program utilizes a three-step reporting system of each event so that no episode of aggression is overlooked. As a first step, the charge nurse is mandated to call for the ASAP team by contacting the hospital switchboard. Secondly, a full incident report is written about the incident. Thirdly, every episode on violence on any shift is also required to be reported at daily nursing rounds. Since the ASAP team members themselves can monitor episodes of violence on their units, they become an additional safeguard against underreporting.

Administrators also need to consider power and influence issues that may arise with the introduction of a new service. To whom do ASAP team members report for ASAP-related responsibilities? To whom do they report for non-ASAP related work matters? To whom does the ASAP team and its leader report to on these matters? Clear and specific answers to these questions will curtail power struggles and attempts at sabotage later on. Administrators may also want to draw up an agency policy governing the accompanying of employee victims by ASAP team members to offsite health care facilities in emergencies.

Finally, with the recent promulgation by the Occupational Safety and Health Administration for health care and social service agencies (OSHA; 1996), senior managers will want to familiarize themselves with other basic risk management strategies for ensuring worksite safety.

*Unions.* Unions understandably have their own concerns for their members. They need to understand that ASAP membership is truly voluntary, that ASAP procedures will not be used by management as some form of employee evaluation system, and that an ASAP program creates a more safe and supportive work environment for their members. Since ASAP team members receive no overtime monies, this issue needs to be addressed. As a matter of ASAP policy, the only type of inkind compensation is flex time or comp time, and this applies only in those cases where the employee returns to the hospital in off-shift hours to do a needed debriefing. In these circumstances the employee is given compensatory time equivalent to the length of the actual debriefing, including travel time. A facility may require that this comp time be used within a thirty day period.

It is important for the ASAP leader to meet with the representatives from all unions in the facility. As with management, the program is explained in detail, questions are answered, and input is sought.

When the first ASAP program was fielded, the union for mental health workers forbade its members to volunteer because there were no overtime ASAP monies. One year later, when we could demonstrate from the aggregate data that was collected that mental health workers were victims in about seventy percent of the cases, the union agreed to let its membership volunteer.

## Legal Matters

Several legal matters will arise before an ASAP team can be fielded. Confidentiality is one of these issues. We have found that staff will view an ASAP program as suspect and possibly a policing agent of the administration, unless the confidentiality of ASAP records can be assured. Management for its part has a responsibility to protect the human rights of both patients and employees. Since ASAP records contain the personal reactions of the employee victim to the act of assault, the needs of both management and employees can be met with the guidelines noted in figure 1. In principle, the full information needed for an incident report is completed by the unit leadership first, so that anyone one who must subsequently evaluate or report on the incident will not be involved in any particular ASAP debriefing. Since ASAP team members must report all crimes, important unreported criminal facts will not be subject to ASAP confidentiality. What remains confidential is the victim's personal reactions about being assaulted. This information never becomes part of an employee's medical or personnel record, and is locked in the ASAP team leader's office. If the employee victim subsequently wants this information for a physician, Industrial Accident Claim, or similar purpose, the employee victim signs an ASAP release of information form in the presence of the ASAP team leader. (See figure 19). After a review of the ASAP notes, the information is forwarded as requested.

A second important legal matter concerns the obtaining of informed consent in the matter of gathering data in the aggregate. In the ASAP program, generic data is obtained without identifying data

# Figure 1

### Guidelines Governing Confidentiality of ASAP Debriefings:

---

1. The ASAP Team person assigned to intervene with a staff member will not be someone who was him/herself a witness or participant. Whenever possible, the assigned ASAP Team person should not be the staff person's supervisor or otherwise be indirectly responsible for the incident which occurred. Since they do not have direct observational information about or responsibility for an incident, they will not generally be subject to any related Internal Affairs Investigation.

2. When the ASAP Team person begins his/her staff intervention, he/she will explicitly advise that as a mandated DPPC reporter, no form of confidentiality would hold, if they discovered that a patient may have been abused or seriously neglected.

3. The ASAP Team personnel are expected to hold in strict confidence any personal information shared by a recipient of their services (except for needed supervision/consultation with other members of the ASAP Team or danger to self/ other situations).

4. Data collected and used in the quality evaluation of the project will be free of information which identifies staff. Data provided by hospital administration to Department of Mental Health Central Office will be coded. The ASAP Team leader will retain the identifying information as confidential and will not release it to any party.

---

on the types and times of assaults, characteristics of the employee victims, and the nature of the assailants as can be seen in figure 14. This data is kept in the aggregate and recorded by hand by each team leader to assess potential high-risk assault situations and to determine how best to utilize ASAP services. Since ASAP has grown to ten sites, there is an overall ASAP program director who provides supervision, ongoing training, and data analysis. The anonymous aggregated data by each team leader is handed to the ASAP program director quarterly, and the program director enters this data into a dedicated computer software program written especially for ASAP and open only to the ASAP program director. The data generated from all programs is then returned to each individual team leader. From time to time, this data is reported in anonymous, aggregated form at professional meetings, or in medical or behavioral science journals.

Since it would be problematic to obtain true informed consent at the moment of crisis, ASAP notifies each employee in advance about the collection of anonymous, aggregated data and the employee's right to refuse data collection yet still obtain ASAP services. This is done in writing as the ASAP program is fielded and sent to every employee with the employee's pay check, as can be seen in figure 5.

A third legal matter may involve the hospital's or agency's policy regarding employees pressing charges against patients. While the published literature (Flannery et al., 1994) suggests that the majority of assaults committed by patients do not occur while they are in psychotic states, the ASAP program takes no advocacy position pro or con. It is there to provide support. However, the hospital needs to have some legally sound policy to guide its employees. If the policy permits employee victims to pursue legal redress as a function of their basic civil rights, these employee victims may find that the courts' gatekeepers refuse to accept these cases. In such cases, we have found education about patient violence and victim trauma to be of assistance in helping the court gatekeeper to understand the nature of such matters.

Since the ASAP program provides clinically-based crisis counseling procedures, it is important that each ASAP team member be covered by some form of group malpractice insurance for all ASAP-related duties. If a number of agencies have banded together to form one team, it is important to be sure that the malpractice insurance of each agency covers any ASAP services provided to employees of the other participating agencies. In practice, we have not found this to be a problem.

# Figure 2

## ASAP Agreement for Interagency Participation:

### URBAN HOSPITAL

#### *The Assaulted Staff Action Program (ASAP)*
#### Interagency Agreement

**To:** _____
                      *ASAP Team Leader*

**From:**   **Agency A**
            **Agency B**
            **Agency C**

**RE:**     **ASAP Team Participation**

**Date:**    _____

      We agree to contribute _____ ASAP volunteers for this project, and will abide by all ASAP policies, procedures, and training initiatives.

      We have determined that our malpractice insurance will cover our own agency's members as they provide ASAP services to the staff of the other participating agencies listed above.

      We agree to participate in the program for a minimum of _____ years.


_____
                      *Agency A*


_____
                      *Agency B*


_____
                      *Agency C*

A final legal matter involves any needed interagency agreements. If agencies have come together, there needs to be some participating agreement in which the parties agree to provide ASAP services to each other's members, to follow ASAP protocols and training procedures, and to participate for a certain minimum period of time. Figure 2 provides one sample agreement.

In all of these legal matters, the ASAP team leader and hospital management should seek the active involvement of counsel to be assured that these matters are properly addressed for a particular ASAP program in a particular facility.

### Financial Matters

While ASAP programs pay for themselves in time (see chapter six), there are start-up costs. These include two page-beepers, paper supplies, and the use of the inhouse mail system to reach all employees.

Administrators will need to think through the issue of ward coverage, when the ASAP team member is off the unit and onsite elsewhere in the facility for a debriefing. In practice, other patient-care site staff usually cover for ASAP employees, when they are off the unit for an hour. These employees understand that the ASAP program is there for them as well as everyone else. However, a formal policy could be promulgated for an individual facility.

Lastly, while we have noted the ASAP standard of practice for comp time earlier, each facility should review the standard for its suitability for a particular facility, or design a policy to meet their agency's specific needs.

Approximate budget allocations should be made in these early stages so that the team can be fielded smoothly on its start date.

### 2. DESIGNING THE TEAM

When administrative matters are in place, the ASAP task force or ASAP team leader turns attention to designing a team to meet the needs of a specific facility. Several steps need to be addressed before the actual design will emerge, and input from senior managers needs to be considered at each step.

The first consideration is how many sites are to be served. It is important that all sites and all shifts be included from the beginning, or some excluded facility members may perceive themselves to be second-class citizens. It is better to start with reduced services for everyone, and then add additional services rather than to exclude some sites initially. In these latter cases, ASAP expansion is resisted.

How many sites are to be served? What hours is each type of site open? How distant are sites from one another? A facility with all of its sites within one building or on grounds within walking distance will design a team differently from an organization that covers twenty-five programs in six different towns. The answer to these questions helps to shape the final team design.

Next, the ASAP team leader or task force will need to know how many employees are in the system, and something of the nature of their work. A facility that has one hundred employees will require a team that is different in scope from a facility with a thousand employees. If there is a greater percentage of a class of employees known to be at higher risk, an ASAP program may require more staffing, even if the actual total number of employees is smaller. For example, in a state hospital setting, less senior, less formally educated mental health workers are at increased risk for assault. If a facility has a large percentage of less senior mental health workers on staff, the probability of assault and the need for ASAP debriefings is increased.

Thirdly, the ASAP design group will want to identify the types of different crimes that are occurring and the frequency of each type. While there are occasional robberies and attempted rapes, the primary type of violence in a state hospital is assault. When the assaults or other types of violence are identified, they need to be clearly defined. Data on their actual occurrence then needs to be tabulated for thirty or sixty days to determine the true frequency of violent events. This data serves as a baseline for comparison, when an ASAP program is fielded.

When we are recording the frequency of assaults for a mental health facility, we use the format in figure 3. This report form has clear definitions of the types of violence that are to be reported and a simple method for recording each incident. The date, time, type or assault (by code number) and the employee's signature are all that is needed. By intent, this report form requires minimal compliance so that accuracy of key data is tabulated. This report form is taken by the ASAP team leader to each unit.

# Figure 3

## ASAP: Assault Baserate Report Form:

**URBAN HOSPITAL**

**ASAP - THE ASSAULTED STAFF ACTION PROGRAM**

UNIT:  _____

WEEK OF:  April 10 - 16, 1994

| | DATE | TIME | TYPE OF ASSAULTS (Code #1-4) | SIGNATURE |
|---|---|---|---|---|
| 1. | | | | |
| 2. | | | | |
| 3. | | | | |
| 4. | | | | |
| 5. | | | | |
| 6. | | | | |
| 7. | | | | |
| 8. | | | | |
| 9. | | | | |
| 10. | | | | |
| 11. | | | | |
| 12. | | | | |
| 13. | | | | |
| 14. | | | | |
| 15. | | | | |
| 16. | | | | |
| 17. | | | | |
| 18. | | | | |
| 19. | | | | |
| 20. | | | | |

**Definitions of Assaults:**
1. Physical Assaults:  Violent acts of unwanted physical contact towards others (slapping, pushing, kicking, spitting, punching, biting, scratching, deliberately throwing an object at a staff member, drawing a lethal weapon on a staff member).
2. Sexual Assault:  Unwanted sexual acts toward staff (unwanted embraces, touching, rape, fondling, exposure).
3. Nonverbal Intimidation:  Nonverbal, non-interpersonal acts meant to frighten staff (throwing an object but not at a person, pounding doors, punching walls, stalking).
4. Verbal Threat:  Verbal statements of intended harm meant to frighten staff (threats to harm person, property, or family).

The team concept is explained to the staff on each unit as well as the importance of establishing baseline accuracy of the level of violence for which ASAP services will be needed. Data is tabulated on each patient-care site weekly for four weeks. The ASAP team leader brings a new form for each week in person to each patient-care site to begin to increase awareness of ASAP, to enhance unit compliance, and to answer any questions that may have arisen. At the end of four weeks, the total number of assaults is tabulated for each type of violence, and for all acts of violence collectively.

The final piece of information in designing the team is to assess the types and numbers of potential assailants. ASAP team leaders need to research the known characteristics of the types of assailants that are being encountered in the facility. As we have noted, in mental health care, younger male patients with a diagnosis of psychosis or other neurological abnormality and histories of substance abuse and violence toward others are more prone to violence. If a facility has a large number of patients with these characteristics, the probability of assault increases dramatically and so will the need for ASAP services.

With this information in hand, the specific design of a team can begin. For example, state hospitals usually have all of their sites on grounds, have several hundred employees with some junior mental health workers, have an episode of an assault a day, and frequently have a patient population that is prone to assault. ASAP teams for these types of facilities usually need eleven line staff, three supervisors, and one team leader, as we discussed earlier. Coverage can be addressed by having one ASAP person on-call for a twenty-four-hour period, for a week at a time, or by having one person on-call for each of the three shifts. More frequent episodes of violence should be expected on those units with more aggressive patients and the least senior mental health workers.

The needs of community programs differ markedly in our experience. Episodes of violence are usually less frequent because the most aggressive patients are hospitalized and patients in the community usually have better coping skills. In these cases, one ASAP team member has been assigned to coverage for one week at a time. Since community programs tend to have multiple sites, community ASAP team members need to have access to safe, affordable, private or public transportation.

Shelters present a different need.  They are primarily open at night, have many less seasoned staff, and their patient population is largely unknown and often intoxicated.  Again, a shelter program may have several sites.  In these circumstances, an ASAP team consisting of two members on-call at the same time might be the better solution.  This is especially true if frequent travel between sites at night is needed.

These types of health care community programs can include both public and private vendors, and usually need less intensive staffing, but staffing for longer periods of time.  Interagency agreements (figure 2) may be required.

The number of sites, the distance between sites, the number of staff, the frequency of violent events, and the known characteristics of the assailants are the basic factors in team design for all types of organizations.  Again, some examples.  A school system could easily garner this needed information.  How many schools are there in the district?  What types of violence can be tabulated?  Which students and teachers are most at risk?  What type of student is likely to commit these crimes?  This basic information would allow any school system to design an ASAP team for its own needs.  If one school has several thousand students, it might warrant its own inhouse ASAP team drawn from its own faculty.  Less frequent episodes of violence in a number of schools might suggest a mobile ASAP team with ASAP members from the faculties of each participating school.

A similar evaluative process could be developed for corrections.  Like the assailants in schools, there is a published literature about which inmates are prone to violence (Flannery, 1995).  An assessment of the number of corrections facilities to be served, and the types and frequency of violence readily lends itself to ASAP team design for corrections facilities.  These teams could address the needs of corrections only, or could be expanded to include the police and courts, in addition to the prisons.

Corporate/industrial settings are another example of sites where an ASAP program could prove helpful.  Industries such as banking, transportation, delivery services, hotel/motels, grocery and liquor stores, gas stations, and taxi cab companies are all at risk for robbery and accompanying acts of assault.  For example, having an ASAP team for all branches of convenience stores in one city could be created to address the needs of sales personnel who have been robbed. Similarly, a number of small and differing businesses in one town could form an interagency team to address the needs of a variety of employee victims at different worksites.

If there is violence, there are victims and usually psychological trauma. An ASAP program can be designed to meet these needs.

## 3. SELECTING THE TEAM
### Team Leaders

One of the more important decisions for the facility is the selection of the ASAP team leader. More than any other factor, the choice of the team leader determines the success of an ASAP team. Good clinical, managerial, and people skills should be considered.

Since ASAP is a crisis intervention clinical service, the team leader needs to have a full understanding of the principles of human development and general clinical practice. Since the leader will also be co-leading CISD debriefings for ward units and co-leading the staff victims' support group, the leader needs to be versed in group dynamics. An understanding of psychological trauma and of possible vicarious traumatization for those who provide services to victims is an additional important asset. The team leader needs to be open to the here-and-now, and directive in utilizing crisis intervention approaches rather than the more common reflective approach of many other types of psychiatric counseling methods. For these several reasons, trained clinicians of any discipline are at a clear advantage as team leaders.

The leader must also be a good manager. The ASAP team leader is responsible for the on-call scheduling of the team and communicating this schedule to the switchboard operators, and for making needed changes due to illnesses or vacations of team members. The leader is responsible for the management of all ASAP services, monitoring the quality of these services, conducting the weekly team meetings to review and monitor all incidents of employee victim assault, providing the team's monthly inservice training, and training new ASAP members, when needed. Additionally, the team leader manages the ASAP paperwork. This includes tracking the completion of ASAP team member reports, logging all ASAP responses to incidents, and completing the data collection and systems entry needed for the quality management aspects of the ASAP program.

People skills are a third important consideration. In general, bright team leaders who are sensitive to others do best. Individuals are needed who can provide both leadership and motivation. They need to be able to think clearly in times of crisis, to be able to elicit input from others, and to tactfully implement needed solutions. Team leaders are required at times to make difficult decisions, to set limits on team members and on the facility, and to reject requests for ASAP services that are beyond the scope and resources of an ASAP team. For example, when the presence of an ASAP is known, requests from within the agency for addressing systems or personnel issues unrelated to assault will be made. Agencies external to the hospital, such as the local police, fire, and emergency services units, may request debriefings. While ASAP team members have made decisions at times to include debriefing of the sudden deaths of patients and staff that affect the hospital community, the team leader must act as a gatekeeper to prevent the team from becoming overextended.

As with anything else in a social system, the successful operation of an ASAP team requires a politically sensitive individual who has the respect and support of senior management, and who understands the importance of developing coalitions and resolving potential conflict by creating situations in which each party gains some of what was sought.

Good team leaders have a sense of ownership of the team, its mission, and its members, and creditability within the agency. They have the energy and enthusiasm needed for the task, and are able to build a sense of team spirit. It is best if team leaders have a minimum of four years of experience in health care settings; a more senior, seasoned leader is often more effective. A sense of affection for others and compassion for victims are helpful assets.

To ensure continuity, team leaders are expected to make a minimum two-year commitment to the leadership position. In an era of downsizing, layoffs, and limited staffing, the team leader may want to select a second ASAP-trained person to be the team co-leader. However, it is the nature of the work that one person, the team leader, be ultimately responsible for final team decisions.

## Team Members and Supervisors

A successful ASAP team also depends on the quality of its first line responders and supervisors.

Team members need to have a basic understanding of the psychology of human development and the basic principles of good clinical practice. As with team leaders, team members need to have an interest in psychological trauma and be comfortable with crisis intervention procedures that require immediate intervention and a directive stance of the part of the debriefer.

Team members need to be reliable, conscientious, and interested in helping others, including victims of violence. Individuals who have themselves been victims of violence are welcome to join the team. In our experience, these members are often the most sensitive to the needs of other victims. However, the ASAP program has also found that any personal victimization issues need to be addressed before joining ASAP. In those cases where this has not been done, team members have subsequently experienced personal intrusive symptoms, when responding to ASAP calls, or have made avoidance responses to requests for ASAP team services. In the latter case, the victimized team member may not respond to the call for assistance and report it as a service declined episode.

Teams work best when members are drawn from all disciplines, including management, and reflect the cultural diversity of the workforce to be served. This includes the rendering of bilingual services, if possible. Team members and supervisors need to have a minimum of two years of experience in health care settings. While student trainees are welcome to attend the ASAP trainings and to observe at weekly team meetings, they have not been permitted to be team members who respond to onsite requests. This is done to protect the personal privacy of staff in case the assault on the unit precipitates intrusive memories of past episodes of personal victimization, and to protect the integrity of the student's training experience. Student trainees have themselves been assaulted on occasion, and need to be able to turn to their supervisors for support without having to be concerned that their experiences of assault are undue burdens on the supervisors.

ASAP team supervisors need to meet all of the requirements of team members as outlined above. Additionally, they need to have a working knowledge of group dynamics for when they co-lead the

CISD ward debriefings and the staff victims' support group. Team supervisors drawn from staff development, human resources, or unit nurse supervisor positions have the added advantage of assessing indirect employee victim needs, when they are on the units in their other roles. This permits informal follow-up of employee victim needs, especially in cases where ASAP services were declined and the employee victim subsequently develops the acute symptoms associated with psychological trauma. As with the position of team leader, more senior, more clinically seasoned staff are usually more effective ASAP team supervisors.

All team members need to make a minimum one year commitment to the team. Before they volunteer, they will need to know the amount of time that will be required of them each month, how ward coverage will be addressed in their absence to perform ASAP duties, how they will be trained, and what will be the hospital's policy for comp time.

### Team Supplies

ASAP teams operate with a minimum of needed support. In addition to the page-beepers, paper supplies for records, xeroxing forms, and the use of the inhouse mail system, little is required in addition to administrative sanction for ASAP service calls. Occasionally, there are space needs for team meetings or inservice trainings, but, by and large, ASAP teams are lean, efficient, and cost-effective.

### Team Leader Supervision

Administering an ASAP program is a complex task that requires ongoing advice and support for the team leader. There are at least three possible ways to accomplish this. First, if there is only one ASAP team within travel distance, the ASAP team leader is encouraged to use the expertise of clinicians and managers within the facility. This might be further supplemented by occasional conferences and consultations with specialists in the field of psychological trauma and PTSD, or conference calls to other distant ASAP programs.

If there is more than one team in an area, the team leaders might consider developing some form of peer-supervision to learn from the experience of other leaders in different ASAP agencies.

These teams could include ASAP leaders from the same type of facilities (e.g., five hospitals) or from different types of agencies (e.g., health care, retail sales, transportation).

A third approach is a more formally designated ASAP team leaders meeting that is chaired, and that systematically addresses member agency team needs. The quality of services delivered, the collection of data from each agency, and common management problems can be addressed. In a format such as this, each agency team agrees to follow the common practices of the group as consensus emerges on common tasks.

This somewhat formal structure provides a good model for additional ASAP teams that may come online. The formal structure permits the development of a separate group for beginning teams that can be chaired by the team leader of the established teams and the development of a buddy-buddy system in which the original teams are paired with the new start-up programs. The established team leader assists the novice leader in designing and fielding the team, assists in training, and generally answers any of the questions that may come up as the novice program begins. This approach builds a sense of cohesion, support, and morale amongst all of the participants. This sense of support has proven invaluable as various team leaders have encountered obstacles in their facilities.

Annual ASAP field days for participants of all teams, the recognition of teams and members through awards, yearly certificates of appreciation, individual team anniversary parties, and the like are additional ways to enhance morale.

**Team Coverage**

When the team has been selected, attention is next directed to developing a system for on-call coverage in advance, so that it is ready to be handed out at the end of the training day. The coverage needs to be designed for the unique needs of any facility, and in accordance with its number of team members. Figures 4A, 4B, and 4C present the standard format for Urban Hospital, the moderate size state hospital that has a fifteen member team.

Figure 4A includes eleven letters of the alphabet for the eleven first line responders as well as the numbers one through three for the ASAP supervisors. Each first responder is assigned a letter of the alphabet, and each supervisor, a number.

# Figure 4A

## ASAP Staff Coverage Assignment Codes:

URBAN HOSPITAL

JULY - SEPTEMBER , 1998
ASAP TEAM AND SUPERVISOR CODES

**Team:**

A -

B -

C -

D -

E -

F -

G -

H -

I -

J -

K -

**Supervisors:**

1 -

2 -

3 -

**Back-Up:**

# Figure 4B

## ASAP Three-Month On-Call Assignment Sheet:

| SPVSR | SUN | MON | TUE | WED | THU | FRI | SAT |
|---|---|---|---|---|---|---|---|
| 3 | JULY | 1 G | 2 H | 3 I | 4 J | 5 K | 6 K |
| 1 | 7 K | 8 A | 9 B | 10 C | 11 D | 12 E | 13 E |
| 2 | 14 E | 15 F | 16 G | 17 H | 18 I | 19 J | 20 J |
| 3 | 21 J | 22 K | 23 A | 24 B | 25 C | 26 D | 27 D |
| 1 | 28 D | 29 E | 30 F | 31 G | --- | JULY | --- |
| 2 | --- | AUGUST | | --- | 1 H | 2 I | 3 I |
| 3 | 4 I | 5 J | 6 K | 7 A | 8 B | 9 C | 10 C |
| 1 | 11 C | 12 D | 13 E | 14 F | 15 G | 16 H | 17 H |
| 2 | 18 H | 19 I | 20 J | 21 K | 22 A | 23 B | 24 B |
| 3 | 25 B | 26 C | 27 D | 28 E | 29 F | 30 G | 31 G |
| SEPT 1 | 1 G | 2 H | 3 I | 4 J | 5 K | 6 A | 7 A |
| 2 | 8 A | 9 B | 10 C | 11 D | 12 E | 13 F | 14 F |
| 3 | 15 F | 16 G | 17 H | 18 I | 19 J | 20 K | 21 K |
| 1 | 22 K | 23 A | 24 B | 25 C | 26 D | 27 E | 28 E |
| 2 | 29 E | 30 F | | --- | SEPT | --- | |

# Figure 4C

## Weekly ASAP Team Coverage Sheet:

### URBAN HOSPITAL

### ASAP TEAM For The Week of:      May 5-11, 1997

### TEAM MEMBER (TEAM BEEPER: 1-800-111-1111):

| | | | |
|---|---|---|---|
| Monday | May 5 | - | John Doe |
| Tuesday | May 6 | - | Mary Doe |
| Wednesday | May 7 | - | Walter Doe |
| Thursday | May 8 | - | Louise Doe |
| Friday | May 9 | - | Henry Doe |
| Saturday | May 10 | | |
| Sunday | May 11 | | |

### SUPERVISOR  (Beeper: 1-800-555-5555):

Monday, May 5- Sunday,May 12  -  Helen Jones

ASAP TEAM MEETING FOR THIS WEEK
WILL BE HELD ON:  MONDAY:May 12,
AT 2:00 pm/Staff Development Library

ASAP Team Leader:      Ellen Smith     X 5038

ASAP Report Forms are in Staff Development Office,
(designated) offices, or at operator's switchboard.

Figure 4B outlines a three month on-call schedule using these letters
and numbers. A different letter of the alphabet is assigned for each
day of the week from Monday through Thursday. On Friday,
Saturday, and Sunday, the same letter is used, and that team member
is on-call for the weekend. The next week continues with the next
letter of the alphabet from Monday through Thursday. Again, on

Friday, one letter of the alphabet is utilized for the weekend. This system ensures equitable weekly coverage, and weekend on-call coverage only once every three months. For each week on the schedule, a number is assigned in the first column to indicate the supervisor back-up on-call. The schedule is completed three months in advance so that team members can plan their schedules, other responsibilities, and vacation periods. Team members are permitted to exchange dates of service among themselves, and are expected to notify the team leader so that the leader can alert the hospital switchboard operators to any changes. In cases of scheduling conflicts among the team members, the team leader is the referee.

Figure 4C completes the coverage schedules. This is the weekly ASAP team coverage sheet, and includes the information in figure 4B on a weekly basis. This third coverage sheet serves as a reminder to team members, and is the coverage sheet that is posted at the hospital switchboard.

The weekly team coverage sheet provides the ASAP team leader with an important opportunity to stay in contact with the dispersed team members. ASAP team leaders often write brief informational notes about the program's current functioning, answer any questions in writing that may have been raised by team members, and list which reports have not been turned in. The team leader then delivers these materials in person to provide support and encouragement to the team members.

### 4. TRAINING THE TEAM
When the team members have been selected, the ASAP task force or team leader then focuses attention on step four, the actual training of the team. Thorough training is critical for ensuring that the ASAP services rendered are of the highest quality, and that all ASAP team members adhere to the standards and clinical practice guidelines that have been developed for an ASAP program.

Standards guide team members in understanding what should be done and when this should take place for each ASAP service rendered. Clinical practice guidelines outline how each service should be provided.

An initial ASAP team training spans two days. The first day is a full day training for all team members. During this day, the basics of theory and practice in the areas of violence, psychological trauma, crisis intervention, and the ASAP model are reviewed.  The second day is a half-day training for the ASAP team leaders supervisors in the theory and practice of CISD (Mitchell & Everly, 1996).  During this two day period, team leaders are given additional ongoing instruction in the administrative, record keeping, and data collection aspects of the team leader's role.  All trainings adhere to ASAP standards and clinical practice guidelines.

A detailed presentation of the trainings, the standards and practice guidelines, and all necessary report forms associated with the delivery of ASAP services is the subject matter of the next chapter.

### 5. FIELDING THE TEAM

While the team is being trained, the ASAP task force or leader will want to begin to educate the hospital workforce in understanding psychological trauma and its impact, and the ASAP program as a helpful approach in addressing this aftermath.  Like most citizens in our country in this present age, the workforce will have become habituated to unacceptably high levels of violence, and, again like most of us in the culture, will want to deny and avoid thinking about psychological trauma and its corresponding message of how vulnerable each of us is.

### Educational Matters

Educational efforts need to be clear, concise, and consistent over time.  A good informal way to begin is to talk about the program as it is being developed during the first five steps outlined here.  This informal marketing of the program informs the hospital social system of upcoming change, and generates a helpful expectation that the ASAP program will, in fact, prove to be helpful and not be another bureaucratic burden.  Questions answered informally over these first five months begin to address the cultural resistance about discussing psychological trauma.

These early efforts are supplemented by more formal educational steps as the start date for the ASAP team approaches.  A helpful first step is to distribute flyers about the ASAP program to every employee with their weekly paychecks.  (E-mail can also be utilized.)  Figure 5 presents the standard letter utilized by all ASAP teams, when they start.  It describes the ASAP program, the team's members, services offered, how those services may be accessed, that

# Figure 5

## ASAP Informational Letter for Employees:

**URBAN HOSPITAL**

**ASAP: THE ASSAULTED STAFF ACTION PROGRAM**

### WHAT IS ASAP?
ASAP is a program for all staff who have been assaulted by a patient. An ASAP team member is on call 24-hours a day, seven (7) days a week to help you should you be assaulted. ASAP is a voluntary service, and all information is confidential.

### WHAT DOES THE ASAP TEAM MEMBER DO?
When the ASAP team member arrives, he or she will help you with the usual and understandable responses to being a victim of an assault. Common feelings may include anger, and fear.

The ASAP team member will help you understand the facts of what has occurred, your feelings about the episode, and what will need to happen so that you feel safe to return to your work area. The ASAP team member is your advocate for your psychological needs. (Medical care is at near-by Smith Medical Center.)

### WHAT IF MORE THAN ONE PERSON IS ASSAULTED AT THE SAME TIME?
Your ASAP team member is able to summon immediate help from the ASAP team supervisor, other ASAP team members, and/or the director of the ASAP team.

### WHY THE NEED FOR ASAP?
When human beings are suddenly confronted with situations that are frightening and beyond their control, they become distressed, apprehensive, and feel out of control. Medical research demonstrates that individuals

# Figure 5 (Cont.)

## ASAP Informational Letter for Employees:

who are able to discuss the event and the feelings it produced at that time will cope more effectively with the problem, and get on with their lives without long-lasting fears.

We have volunteered for the project because we believe this to be a needed service for our fellow employees. All staff victim episodes are held in complete confidence.

### WHAT WILL ASAP COST ME?

ASAP is a benefit provided to all Urban Hospital employees by the hospital management. There are no financial costs to the users of this service.

### WHAT FOLLOW-UP IS PROVIDED FOR STAFF VICTIMS?

The ASAP team member will contact each victim by phone or in person three days later, and again in ten days after the incident, to see how the staff member is doing. The ASAP team also provides a weekly support group to help victims discuss the assault, and to master any lingering concerns.

*The ASAP team does not provide personal psychotherapy for staff members' individual issues.* Referrals to private therapists can be arranged, if the assault at work should somehow be related to other events in a person's life.

### WHO ARE THE ASAP TEAM MEMBERS?

We are your colleagues who work here at Urban Hospital.

*For further information, contact:*
ASAP Team Leader:  Ellen Smith X123
Director of Nursing:   John Doe    X456

information is confidential, and the fact that this program is a free employee benefit. This introductory flyer should appear on hospital stationery, and can be modified for individual agency needs. For example, if employees are highly vocal about union involvement, a paragraph could be added to explain the fact of union support and how it was obtained.

These first letters are then followed by informational meetings with all departments, patient-care site team meetings, supervisors' meetings, union meetings, administrator meetings, and any other format that can be utilized for ASAP educational purposes. Meetings should include all interested stakeholders, and all questions should be addressed in full. Flyers with the letters "ASAP" in large type and the team's start date should be distributed and posted on all patient-care sites.

The need for education will continue, and figure 6 presents one approach that has proven helpful. This is an example of a monthly memo to all employees with their paychecks. These memos address any fears about the ASAP program and discuss some aspect of psychological trauma, in this case, the importance of caring attachments. One memo is sent each month, and the list of topics could include psychological trauma; its symptoms; the phases of untreated PTSD; disruptions in mastery, attachment, and meaning; why victim-blaming occurs; why violence does not "come with the turf."

Repeated educational messages have proven helpful in assisting the workforce to understand the nature of psychological trauma and contributed to increased utilization of ASAP services. As these occur, victim-blaming decreases to nil, and a community of compassion is fostered. These educational initiatives are an important component in the successful fielding of an ASAP team.

## Fielding the Team

When the baserate data of step two has been collected, and the first informational flyer for employees has been distributed, a start date is chosen and the team begins its service. Given the current changes in the health care industry with downsizings mergers, and layoffs, every team may not be able to provide all services at the start. As a basic minimum, every team should provide individual crisis interventions; CISD debriefings; and some form of a victims' support

# Figure 6

## ASAP: Follow-Up Educational Memo for Employees:

### URBAN HOSPITAL

**TO:**        All Employees
**FROM:**    Ellen Smith - Director,
                 Assaulted Staff Action Program (ASAP)
                 X123

**DATE:**    October 1, 1990

As we complete our first six months of service, your ASAP colleagues want you to know that we remain on-call 24-hours a day to help you in the event you are assaulted by a patient. We are here to help lessen the psychological distress that can be associated with being assaulted. All ASAP records are held in the strictest confidence, and are not a part of any employee personnel or medical record. We are not monitoring sick leave or Industrial Accident (I.A.) Claims for the hospital's management.

Since our basic program is now in place, ASAP is offering a new service. ASAP is now ready to help any staff victim who was assaulted by a patient prior to our starting date of April 2, 1990. Any employee who was distressed by an episode of patient-inflicted violence prior to April 2nd, is welcome to attend the staff support group any Friday, from 2:00 to 3:00 pm in the Staff Development Library in the Furcolo Building. This is true for employees on I.A. Claims, and sick leave as well as those at work. Everyone is welcome - no appointment is necessary. All group sessions are held in strict confidence.

# Figure 6 (Cont.)

## ASAP: Follow-Up Educational Memo for Employees:

### PSYCHOLOGICAL TRAUMA FROM ASSAULTS AND SUPPORT NETWORKS

When a person is assaulted, one's sense of control, one's support network of friends, and one's ability to make any sense of the assault, may be disrupted. In my memo of August 27, 1990, I discussed the loss of one's sense of control. In this writing, I would like to focus on support networks.

Friends not only make us feel better about ourselves by providing support, companionship, information, and tangible assistance, but are also good for our physical health. Friends stabilize our heart muscle's functioning, and lower both blood pressure and pulse. Friends enhance the capacity of our immune system to fight disease. Friends enhance the circulation of endorphins in our brain, and these endorphins make us feel better and not so blue.

Unfortunately, when people experience psychological trauma, a common first reaction is to pull away from other people, since another person has usually inflicted the harm. It is important to keep the assailant at a safe distance, but, if we withdraw from everyone else too, we lose the benefits mentioned above.

If you are assaulted at work, remember to talk to your colleagues, your family, your friends, and your ASAP team member. Don't withdraw; being with others hastens your recovery.

group, which can be as basic as the ASAP team leader meeting informally with any hospital victim of assault requiring additional support. Whatever services are chosen need to be provided on all shifts and to all participating sites.

As the ASAP program begins, it is important that a senior manager in the hospital mandate that all patient assaults on staff be reported to the ASAP program. Figure 7 presents one method of accomplishing this. Virtually, every ASAP program that has not mandated this reporting from the team's start has faltered, until such mandated reporting is put in place.

A second important consideration relates to the matter of collecting data for quality management and research purposes. These matters require the informed consent of all employees as the ASAP begins. Since it is neither practical nor possible to accurately obtain informed consent in the beginning of an ASAP service immediately after an assault, as we noted earlier, ASAP has developed its own process to insure that informed consent has been obtained. In the ASAP process, all employees are again sent a letter with their paychecks. (See figure 8.) This letter informs the employee of the reasons and steps involved in gathering the data anonymously and in the aggregate for purpose of quality management, research, and publication. It states clearly that any employee may refuse to have data gathered on any particular episode of violent assault, and that this decision will in no way affect the providing of any and all ASAP services. This letter additionally allays staff fears that management may be using the ASAP program for some other unstated reason.

ASAP team leaders should expect resistance when the team is fielded. When the team actually begins to provide service, several issues may emerge. These may include general social system inertia as something new begins, social system paranoia concerning ulterior motives by management, fears of possible further impending layoffs that haven't been discussed, active political efforts by various hospital groups to sabotage the new service, and routine refusals because violence "comes with the turf." These resistances are best addressed in a straight forward manner and clearly, concisely, and factually in writing. (Monthly staff memos to all employees are helpful in this regard.) Challenge the employees outright to find some breech of ASAP confidentially. If the necessary steps noted have been put in place, there will be no such breech. Assess with

# Figure 7

## ASAP Mandated Reporting Memo:

### URBAN HOSPITAL

### MEMORANDUM

TO:    ALL NURSING UNITS
          HEAD NURSES
          CHARGE NURSES

FROM:  Director of Nursing
          Director of Health Services Unit

RE:    **Required Use of ASAP Team**

DATE:  January 2, 1991

Please remember that, when any staff member is assaulted, the ASAP Team <u>must</u> be called, no matter what the hour. It has come to my attention that ASAP has not been contacted at the time of assaults on three (3) occasions in the past two (2) weeks.

This is a service we provide to all employees and they are free to decline the service. However, the nurse in charge is responsible for initiating the call for ASAP service. If the assaulted employee and the ASAP team member feel an immediate site visit is not warranted or wanted, the ASAP member will leave the unit immediately.

My personal thank you for your ongoing involvement in working with this vital hospital program.

cc:   Assistant Directors of Nursing
      Unit Directors
      ASAP Team Leader

# Figure 8

## ASAP Required Informed Consent Letter:

To:        All Staff
From:      ASAP Team Leader
Re:        Assaulted Staff Action Program (ASAP) Update

Date:      April 10, 1995

Periodically, I'd like to take the opportunity to update you on the ASAP Program, both here at Urban and across the state system. Ten facilities have developed ASAP teams and are now involved in responding to assaults on staff.

Our own ASAP Team has been operating since March 6th. In that time we have responded to a number of incidents where staff have been assaulted. As you know, we are operating 24 hours per day and can be accessed through the switchboard operators, who will page the ASAP on-call worker at the request of any staff member or charge nurse.

As for the state-wide program, each month, the ASAP team leaders from each of the participating state hospitals, meet to discuss ways in which we can improve the program. In addition, we are beginning to look at anonymous raw data, ie., number of assaults, types of patients who most frequently assault staff, times of day when staff are most vulnerable to assault, reaction to violence, etc. This raw data is collected anonymously only in the aggregate so there is no way to identify specific staff victims. This data will be analyzed by the ASAP team leaders and by Jane Smith, the Director of the statewide ASAP program. We may also, at some point, write an article about the ASAP program and submit it for publication in a psychiatric journal. If we do, only aggregate data or summaries of the types of situations we have responded to and staff reactions to violence will be used. As always, the confidentiality of each staff member who avails themselves of the ASAP team will be protected. At no time are the names of staff recorded, released or discussed. Any employee victim may refuse to have information collected. This in no way jeopardizes any employee's access to any and all ASAP services.

We hope you will continue to call us, when you yourself or a colleague is assaulted. In the meantime, if you have any question or comments, please feel free to contact the ASAP Team Leader.

management the motivation of any political forces that seek to undermine the program, and attempt to address those issues early on. Although there are any number of common political reasons for resisting ASAP, it is not uncommon to find that some agents of this resistance may, in fact, be victims of untreated PTSD, and are seeking to block the program as a means of maintaining their own avoidance of memories of past, personal moments of victimization.

The experience of most ASAP programs is that persistence pays off. In most cases, there comes a time when the facility faces a true crisis with regards to violence. A major fire on a unit, a particularly gruesome assault, a line-of-duty death. Each of these can present a defining moment for acceptance for an ASAP team. If the educational efforts have been done in advance, and the offering of services, however often declined, has been persistent, ASAP's response to the major event usually marks a turning point in its acceptance, and resistance fades.

A final step in the initial fielding of an ASAP team is to do outreach to those employees who were assaulted before ASAP began and who remain out on sick leave or Industrial Accident (IA) Claims. This outreach must be done sensitively so that employees are not made paranoid by the process. A letter, such as that found in figure 9, is drafted and sent to all employees. Unions can be of important assistance here by calling the injured employees in advance to tell them that this letter is coming and that the union supports its membership through this program.

The team leader is free to meet these assaulted employees, where the employee victims feel most comfortable. The service is explained, the victim's assault is reviewed, and any requested support is provided.

Some employees will not respond, but others will, and the impact of an ASAP debriefing may be particularly helpful in assisting the employee's return to work. Consider the following example.

A young nurse, who was a person of color, was kicked in the stomach by a white male patient. She had been out on leave for several weeks. During that interim, she became the focus of much victim-blaming and racial stereotyping on her unit by her colleagues. During outreach, the ASAP team member learned that the employee had been pregnant and had lost her fetus as a result of the assault

# Figure 9

## ASAP Outreach Letter to Previously Injured Staff:

## URBAN HOSPITAL

October 1, 1990

Dear Urban Hospital Employee:

The Assaulted Staff Action Program (ASAP) is a treatment intervention program provided by your colleagues here at Urban Hospital to help lessen the potential negative impact of being assaulted by a patient. Such assaults can leave any of us feeling frightened, apprehensive, angry, and leave us with a sense of not feeling in control. Talking to an ASAP team member can help to lessen these negative outcomes. All of the services that we provide are held in the strictest confidence, and are not a part of any employee's personnel file or medical record.

Our program has been in place for six months now. It seems helpful to employees who have been assaulted by patients, and we on the ASAP team would like to extend those benefits to any employee assaulted before we started on April 2, 1990. This new service is specifically for employees currently at work, but who were assaulted before April 2nd, as well as any staff who are on sick leave or Industrial Accident (I.A.) Claim for an assault-related injury before April 2nd. We are here to provide counseling for the psychological effects of being assaulted, and we in ASAP are not attempting to monitor sick leave or I.A. Claims for the hospital's management.

Jane Doe, RN, and I run a staff victims' support group on Friday afternoons from 2:00 to 3:00 PM. Everyone is welcome, no appointment is necessary, and, as I have noted above, all group sessions are held in strict confidence.

Some of you may receive this letter at home because of I.A. Claims or sick leave. You are receiving this letter because I asked Human Resources to provide me with a list of our Urban colleagues on leave because they were assaulted in the line of duty. No one in hospital management will know whether you come or not, and this is the only letter you will receive from me. This letter's sole purpose is to inform you of our newly expanded ASAP service for all staff victims. The ASAP team is now available for you, if you wish it to be so.

Enclosed is a more detailed flyer about ASAP. Do talk to your colleagues here at the hospital about ASAP's work, contact your union shop steward, call me if I can be of further help, and do feel free to drop by any Friday afternoon for the above mentioned support group. We are here to serve you.

Sincerely,


ASAP Team Leader (X123)
Enclosure

(fully documented in a nearby general hospital medical record). She had become seriously depressed, and now was fearful of returning to the unit because the same patient was still in residence. The employee lived alone, and had had no one to discuss the assault with except her father out of state who insisted that she resign. The employee was reluctant to do this as she cared for her work and her patients.

Several ASAP interventions were drawn up. The employee had repeated individual ASAP debriefings, until she resolved the personal issues raised for her by the assault. A meeting with the unit management was arranged with the employee and the ASAP team leader present. During this meeting, the loss of the fetus was shared. The management and staff's shame was palpable. Victim-blaming and racial stereotyping stopped, and calls of support to the employee's residence were forthcoming. As a final step in assisting the employee's actual return to the worksite, the ASAP team leader provided another common ASAP intervention, when employees are afraid to return to the unit. The team leader met the employee at the unit door, and accompanied the employee onto the unit. He remained there for two hours with the employee, until she was desensitized to her fears and felt safe enough to continue on her own.

Outreach can be extremely helpful.

In closing this section, ASAP has found it important to not begin fielding an ASAP team during the summer months because staff are on vacation and an understanding of the ASAP services is impeded. Similarly, it does not appear helpful to field an ASAP team before a major layoff or downsizing process is to occur. ASAP programs that are in place prior to a downsizing can be helpful in addressing the potential concomitant increase inpatient assaults (Flannery, Hanson, Penk, Pastva, Navon, & Flannery, 1997). However, to begin an ASAP program under circumstances of major facility change only adds to the confusion.

## Data Collection

The last step in fielding a team is to begin the ongoing process of data collection for purposes of quality management and research on the problems encountered when studying violence and its treatment interventions.

Each facility will want to design its own system of data

collection, depending on its resources. At a very minimum, the total number of assaults should be recorded so that it can be compared to the facility's baserate data that was collected before ASAP was fielded. The fielding of an ASAP program may result in no effect on the overall assault rate, in a decline in the assault rate, or an increase in the assault rate. If the latter outcome is obtained, the ASAP team leader and hospital management must evaluate this finding to be sure that ASAP is not somehow making matters worse. This outcome has not happened to date.

A second basic minimum in data collection requires some form of evaluation of the ASAP services to be assured that the ASAP services themselves are not harmful to employee victims. A variety of formal assessment procedures could be employed, but, at the very least, self-reports should be obtained from debriefed employee victims.

Figures 10 through 14 present a series of increasingly sophisticated data collection forms. Figure 10 provides for the basic collection of simple data that any ASAP team would need. Figure 11 through 13 increase the complexity of the data gathered, and include data sheets that permit a full year's oversight of the team's services.

Figure 14 outlines the most sophisticated data collection form, and is the one currently in use by all ASAP teams in Massachusetts. This form provides rich data on the nature of violence in the participating facilities statewide as well as in each individual facility. This data base permits an evaluation of ASAP services, the characteristics of the employee victims, and the characteristics of those patients that are assaultive. Such data permits us to monitor the quality of services provided, to deploy resources where they are needed, and to alert all staff to the categories of high-risk patients. Such data may also be helpful in applying for grant funding to obtain additional resources for further treatment interventions or ongoing research.

It would be helpful if new ASAP programs in other states adopted the data collection process in figure 14. This would permit the evaluation of the ASAP program in other settings, in other states, and the ability to compare findings across settings could lead to ongoing improvements in participating ASAP programs and in our understanding of violence in general.

This concludes our overview of the steps needed to successfully field an ASAP program. Again, this chapter contains a good deal of information, and the implementation of a team should be done over a period of time. There are no specific time constraints on how long each step should take, but, in general, they should proceed in the sequence noted here, and at a pace that does not overwhelm the ASAP task force or team leader.

In the next chapter, we turn our attention to the matters of step four, training the team. We examine in detail the important educational process necessary for developing competent ASAP service providers.

# Figure 10

## Basic ASAP Weekly Report Form:

**URBAN HOSPITAL**

**ASAP INCIDENT LOG**

| Date | Name of Employee or Victim | Name of Assaultive Patient | Ward |
|---|---|---|---|
|  |  |  |  |
|  |  |  |  |
|  |  |  |  |
|  |  |  |  |
|  |  |  |  |
|  |  |  |  |
|  |  |  |  |
|  |  |  |  |
|  |  |  |  |
|  |  |  |  |
|  |  |  |  |

# Figure 11

## ASAP Weekly Report Form:

### URBAN HOSPITAL
### ASAP WEEKLY REPORT FORM

| DATE | DAY OF WEEK | M/F | STAFF VICTIM | REFUSE | ASAP MEMBER | PATIENT | VIOL. TYPE | WARD | SHIFT | INJURY | STAFF REST-RAINT | GROUP | FAMILY |
|---|---|---|---|---|---|---|---|---|---|---|---|---|---|
| | | | | | | | | | | | | | |
| | | | | | | | | | | | | | |
| | | | | | | | | | | | | | |
| | | | | | | | | | | | | | |
| | | | | | | | | | | | | | |
| | | | | | | | | | | | | | |
| | | | | | | | | | | | | | |
| | | | | | | | | | | | | | |
| | | | | | | | | | | | | | |
| | | | | | | | | | | | | | |
| | | | | | | | | | | | | | |
| | | | | | | | | | | | | | |
| | | | | | | | | | | | | | |

# Figure 12

## Basic ASAP Monthly Report Form:

**URBAN HOSPITAL**
**ASAP MONTHLY REPORTS - 1991-92**

| *MONTH* | APRIL | MAY | JUNE | JULY | |
|---|---|---|---|---|---|
| CALLS | | | | | |
| REFUSED CALLS | | | | | |
| DAYS IN MONTH | | | | | |
| TOTAL ASSAULTS | | | | | |

| *MONTH* | AUGUST | SEPTEMBER | OCTOBER | NOVEMBER | |
|---|---|---|---|---|---|
| CALLS | | | | | |
| REFUSED CALLS | | | | | |
| DAYS IN MONTH | | | | | |
| TOTAL ASSAULTS | | | | | |

| *MONTH* | DECEMBER | JANUARY | FEBRUARY | MARCH | |
|---|---|---|---|---|---|
| CALLS | | | | | |
| REFUSED CALLS | | | | | |
| DAYS IN MONTH | | | | | |
| TOTAL ASSAULTS | | | | | |

# Figure 13

## More Detailed ASAP Monthly Report:

### URBAN HOSPITAL
### ASAP-ASSAULTED STAFF DATA

Date:  December, 1995
ASAP TEAM: URBAN HOSPITAL

Total number of  assaults:          _____

Total number of Assaults by gender:        Employees (Female): _____
                                           Employees (Male):    _____

Total Number of assaults by discipline:
      Nurses:  _____       Social Workers:  _____      MD:    _____
      MHW's: _____        Psychologists:  _____       Other:  _____

Number of assaults each month:
(1=Physical, 2=Sexual, 3=Non-Verbal, 4=Verbal):

| Jan, 1997 | | Feb, 1997 | | Mar, 1997 | | Apr, 1997 | | May, 1997 | | Jun, 1997 | |
|---|---|---|---|---|---|---|---|---|---|---|---|
| Type 1: | | Type 1: | | Type 1: | | Type 1: | | Type 1: | | Type 1: | |
| Type 2: | | Type 2: | | Type 2: | | Type 2: | | Type 2: | | Type 2: | |
| Type 3: | | Type 3: | | Type 3: | | Type 3: | | Type 3: | | Type 3: | |
| Type 4: | | Type 4: | | Type 4: | | Type 4: | | Type 4: | | Type 4: | |
| Total: | | Total: | | Total: | | Total: | | Total: | | Total: | |

| Jul, 1997 | | Aug, 1997 | | Sep, 1997 | | Oct, 1997 | | Nov, 1997 | | Dec, 1997 | |
|---|---|---|---|---|---|---|---|---|---|---|---|
| Type 1: | | Type 1: | | Type 1: | | Type 1: | | Type 1: | | Type 1: | |
| Type 2: | | Type 2: | | Type 2: | | Type 2: | | Type 2: | | Type 2: | |
| Type 3: | | Type 3: | | Type 3: | | Type 3: | | Type 3: | | Type 3: | |
| Type 4: | | Type 4: | | Type 4: | | Type 4: | | Type 4: | | Type 4: | |
| Total: | | Total: | | Total: | | Total: | | Total: | | Total: | |

# Figure 14

## Preferred ASAP Data Collection Report Form:

The table has the following column headers (VICTIM / DATE):

Hospital Group Number; Staff Victim Number; Job Block; Sex of Staff Victim; Unit; Shift; Time of Day (Use 24 hour time: ie: 1530 for 4:30pm); Day of the Week; Date of Assault - Month; Date of Assault - Day; Date of Assault - Year; Prior ASAP contact? (yes /no /unknown ); Refused ASAP contact? (yes/no); ASAP Team member; Type of Assault; Injuries; Restraint and Seclusion (yes/no); Staff group; Ward CISD; Family Counseling; Sick Leave Days; IA Claim Days

Rows numbered 1–10.

**ASAP PROGRAM NUMBERS**
1 - Hospital "A"
2 - CMHC "B"
3 -
4 -
5 -
6 -
7 -
8 -
9 -
10 -
11 -
12 -
13 -
14 -
15 -

Month/Year:

**JOB BLOCK**
1 - MHW
2 - RN
3 - LPN
4 - Psychologist
5 - REC Therapist
6 - Social Worker
7 - Psychiatrist
8 - OT Therapist
9 - Lab Tech
10 - MD
11 - RC
12 - House Manager
13 - Case Manager
14 - Clinician
15 - Allied Mental Health
16 - Support Staff (ie: housekeeping, clerical)
17 - Student
18 - OTHER

**SHIFT**
1 - 7A-3P
2 - 3P-11P
3 - 11P-7A

**DAY OF WEEK**
1 - Sunday
2 - Monday
3 - Tuesday
4 - Wednesday
5 - Thursday
6 - Friday
7 - Saturday

**GENDER CODES**
1 - Female
2 - Male

**PRIMARY DIAGNOSIS OF PATIENT**
1 - Schizophrenia
2 - Bipolar Disorder
3 - Major Depressive Episod
4 - Personality Disorder
5 - Substance Abuse Only
6 - Organic Brain Dysfunction
7 - Other - Specify

**Patient History of Violence as a Victim**
0 - No
1 - Yes
2 - Unknown

**YES / NO questions**
0 - no
1 - yes

# Figure 14 (continued)

## Preferred ASAP Data Collection Report Form:

| First Response | | | | | | Second Encounter | | | | | | Third Encounter | | | | | | ASSAULTIVE PATIENT | | | | | | | |
|---|---|---|---|---|---|---|---|---|---|---|---|---|---|---|---|---|---|---|---|---|---|---|---|---|---|
| Mastery | Attachments | Meaning | Physical Symptoms | Intrusive Symptoms | Avoidant Symptoms | Mastery | Attachments | Meaning | Physical Symptoms | Intrusive Symptoms | Avoidant Symptoms | Mastery | Attachments | Meaning | Physical Symptoms | Intrusive Symptoms | Avoidant Symptoms | Sex | Age | Primary Diagnosis | Substance Abuse(@ time of assault) | Substance Abuse(past history) | History of Violence towards Other | History of Violence as Victim | History of Sexual Abuse |
| | | | | | | | | | | | | | | | | | | | | | | | | | |
| | | | | | | | | | | | | | | | | | | | | | | | | | |
| | | | | | | | | | | | | | | | | | | | | | | | | | |
| | | | | | | | | | | | | | | | | | | | | | | | | | |
| | | | | | | | | | | | | | | | | | | | | | | | | | |
| | | | | | | | | | | | | | | | | | | | | | | | | | |
| | | | | | | | | | | | | | | | | | | | | | | | | | |
| | | | | | | | | | | | | | | | | | | | | | | | | | |
| | | | | | | | | | | | | | | | | | | | | | | | | | |
| | | | | | | | | | | | | | | | | | | | | | | | | | |
| | | | | | | | | | | | | | | | | | | | | | | | | | |

**NARRATIVE DESCRIPTION OF INJURIES & ACTIONS**

ASAP INJURY CODE
1 - Soft tissue injury
   (with/without swelling)
2 - Head or back injury
3 - Bone/tendon/ligament injury
4 - Open wounds
   (scratches/bites/spitting)
5 - Abdominal trauma
6 - Psychological fright
   (no apparent injury

1 _____
2 _____
3 _____
4 _____
5 _____
6 _____
7 _____
8 _____
9 _____
10 _____

DESCRIPTION OF ASSAULT
1 - Physical Assault
2 - Sexual Assault
3 - Nonverbal Intimidation
4 - Verbal Threats

# Chapter

# 4

## ASAP: TRAINING AND STANDARDS

*Help me make it through the night.*
- Daniel Berrigan

*You have to study a great deal to know a little.*
- Montesquieu

Delores walked through the metal detector at the door of PS 777, and headed toward the teachers' room.

She looked dreadful this morning and she knew it. She had bandaged her left arm quickly as best as she could, and she now hoped that no blood had seeped through her long sleeve blouse on her way to work. Pain was her constant companion, but the vice-like grip in her left arm was immobilizing, even for her.

"You look like hell." Rebecca, her fellow seventh grade teacher, was nothing, if not brutally frank. "What happened?"

"Oh, nothing, really. I was up with little Benedict through the night."

Benedict. Her Benedict.

She and Victor had had a tolerable marriage, until the birth of their son, Benedict, nearly two years ago. Victor had always had a nasty temper, and had occasionally slapped and pushed her, but the birth of their son was a turning point in the dehumanizing of human life.

Even she was startled at what she had been through in two short years. Victor's weapons had included unspeakably ugly words, forced anal intercourse, cigarette burns, frying pans, scalding water, pool cues, golf clubs, telephone cords, razors, knives. Anything handy. She had told no one. Who would have believed it?

As she prepared to leave the teacher's room for class, Victor came through the door in a white rage, and continued the beating of his wife that he had begun earlier that morning. Rebecca froze in fear, and, then, instinctively grabbed Victor's arm in an attempt to stop the fighting. She found herself on the ground with Victor's hands on her throat. She somehow squirmed loose, only to find herself slammed hard into a bookcase on the other side of the room.

"Police." "Freeze." Victor was arrested and taken away in handcuffs.

Both of the teachers were in tears. Rebecca's back seared with pain, and Delores's left arm was bleeding profusely. Yesterday, Victor had slashed her arm with a knife. The gash required eighteen sutures to close it. This morning at 4:00 A.M., in a drunken rage, Victor had pulled out the sutures with a pair of pliers. One . . . by one . . . by one . . . by one . . . .

Victor — from the Latin: Conqueror

Delores — from the Spanish: Sorrows

Benedict — from the Latin: Blessed

Rebecca — from the Hebrew: Noose

Many of us tend to think of domestic violence as occurring only in the home, but, in fact, it is found in worksites and community streets as assailants stalk their spousal prey, and continue the violence, when they find them. Rebecca is an example of an innocent bystander caught up in domestic violence in the workplace. Her body in pain, her mind in fear, she could appreciably benefit from an ASAP debriefing, and, as we have just seen, such a team for the students and teachers of a school system could be readily designed and fielded. The quality of the ASAP services that would be rendered would depend upon the ASAP team members being adequately trained. There is no substitute for excellence in training in the pursuit of high quality care.

This chapter outlines those ASAP training procedures in detail, and lists the standards of performance and the clinical practice guidelines upon which an ASAP program is based. These factors are key components in an ASAP program so that team members can provide helpful remediation and do no harm. We turn first to training.

## ASAP TRAINING

### ASAP First Line Responders

*Content*

The ASAP training process is based on a body of knowledge that informs all ASAP services. It focuses on the general nature of violence, violence specific to health care worksites, psychological trauma, principles of crisis intervention, and the ASAP approach, matters addressed earlier in this book. This content is drawn from four books: *Violence in America: Coping with Drugs, Distressed Families, Inadequate Schooling and Acts of Hate* (Flannery, 1997); *Violence in the Workplace* (Flannery, 1995); *Post-Traumatic Stress Disorder: The Victim's Guide to Healing and Recovery* (Flannery 1992, 1989); and *Critical Incident Stress Debriefing (CISD): An Operation's Manual for the Prevention of Traumatic Stress Among Emergency Services and Disaster Workers* (Mitchell & Everly, 1996), and one journal article on crisis intervention principles (Sandoval, 1985).

Each team is encouraged to obtain a copy of each book and to circulate them among team members. In addition, each team receives an ASAP training manual that includes a description of the program, policies and procedures, and all necessary blank forms. This is supplemented with a second manual that contains fifty articles with relevant information about psychological trauma and trauma interventions. Both manuals are in binder format so that procedures and reprints can be updated as necessary.

The day begins with team-building, and a review of the materials on violence, trauma, and ASAP. Interspersed role-playing situations that illustrate the content material are arranged throughout the training day in increasing levels of complexity. In the first role-play, team members pair off in twos, and take turns being the ASAP first responder debriefing the victim.

The next role-plays are done in groups, and are based on real episodes of assault in the hospital. (See below for examples.) The first responders are divided into two teams. Some members volunteer to role-play victims. The others are asked to leave the room, while the role-play is put in place. During this time the others choose one of their number to be the ASAP team debriefer. The remaining members of each group act as "advisors" to the ASAP debriefer, and offer suggestions on how to approach any given act of assault most effectively. Advisors can also be pressed into ASAP service, if the team leader determines extra assistance is needed, when he or she arrives onsite at the role-play. All role-plays take place on mats for safety and cleanliness.

Role-plays include employee victims ranging from distraught employees in severe agitation, to those mute from fear, to those who are deceased. Scenes are made as real as possible, and include things such as draping the body of the deceased, using ketchup to connote blood on the faces of injured employees, and having furniture in disarray. The goal is to facilitate learning, and to desensitize team members now to situations they may actually encounter on the unit. When the scene is ready, the team members in the hall return to the room, and the ASAP designated team leader begins the debriefing. All team members are reminded to ensure safety first, to obtain needed medical attention, and not to touch an employee victim without requesting permission from the victim. Victims understandably may be experiencing boundary problems, and being touched suddenly in the confusion by a relatively unknown ASAP team member may cause additional distress. ASAP team members should state clearly who they are and why they are there.

The CISD role-plays proceed in a similar fashion. However, in these cases, all team members remain in the room and volunteer to be the ASAP supervisory debriefers, the principle victims, and other staff, administrators, and patient members of the community.

*The Training Days*

Figures 15 and 16 outline the ASAP training days for first responders and ASAP supervisors.

The days begin with a continental breakfast so that the team members can begin the process of bonding as a group, and the day itself begins with welcoming remarks by the chief executive officer and other senior managers, so that team members understand the importance of the mission and its full support by management.

As can be seen in figure 15, the program covers the topic areas of ASAP, violence, psychological trauma, individual crisis interventions (Sandoval, 1985), CISD, and ASAP administrative procedures as the day proceeds. Role-plays highlight needed skills.

# Figure 15

## ASAP Training Day: First Responders:

### URBAN HOSPITAL

### ASAP: ASSAULTED STAFF ACTION PROGRAM
### TRAINING PROGRAM:  MARCH 28, 1990

I. Opening:  Continental Breakfast      8:30 - 9:00

II. Introductory Remarks:  Chief Operating Officer      9:00 - 9:15

III. What is ASAP?      9:15 - 9:45

IV. The Nature of Violence and Psychological Trauma      9:45 - 10:30
     (A) Symptoms
     (B) The Role of Mastery, Attachment, and Meaning

**COFFEE BREAK**

V. Role-playing I: Interviewing the Victim      10:40 - 11:00

VI. Principles of Crisis Intervention      11:00 - 11:30

VII. Role-Playing II: Interviewing the Victim on the Ward      11.30 - 12:00

**LUNCH**

I. Critical Incident Stress Debriefing      1:00 - 1:30

II. Role-Playing III: CISD:
     Complicated Victim Situations      1:30 - 2:30

III. The ASAP Program and ASAP Record Keeping      2:30 - 3:25

**COFFEE BREAK**

IV. Administrative Issues/Relaxation Exercises      3:30 - 4:15

V. Wrap-up      4:15 - 5:00

# Figure 16A

## ASAP Training Day: ASAP Supervisors:

### URBAN HOSPITAL

### ASAP: ASSAULTED STAFF ACTION PROGRAM
### TRAINING DAY FOR ASAP SUPERVISORS

| I. | Critical Incident Stress Debriefing (CISD) | 9:00 - 10:00 |
| II. | Role-Play I: CISD on the Ward Unit | 10:00 - 10:45 |

**COFFEE BREAK**

| III. | Role-Play II: Advanced CISD: Complicated Situations | 11:00 - 12:00 |

Luncheon is supplied as a courtesy by the facility, and the program closes with relaxation exercises that team members can employ to minimize stress and burnout. [See Appendix B (Flannery, 1995)]. Near the end of the day, the ASAP training instructor turns the program over to the ASAP team leader, who reviews scheduling, the beeper system, the roles of various members, ASAP documentation procedures, comp time policy, and team meetings. The day closes with the presentation of graduation certificates (figure 20).

The second training is a half-day program for ASAP supervisors. It includes a review of the steps of CISD, based on the work of Drs. Mitchell and Everly (1996), and role-plays of common situations where CISD might be needed.

These two trainings may be done sequentially or spaced over time, as staffing needs dictate.

*Examples of Role-Playing*

Below are listed some of the more common examples of individual crisis counseling and CISD role-plays that ASAP trainings

# Figure 16B

## ASAP Training Day (CISD): ASAP Supervisors:

### URBAN HOSPITAL

### ASAP: ASSAULTED STAFF ACTION PROGRAM

**Critical Incident Stress Debriefing:**

<u>Introduction</u>

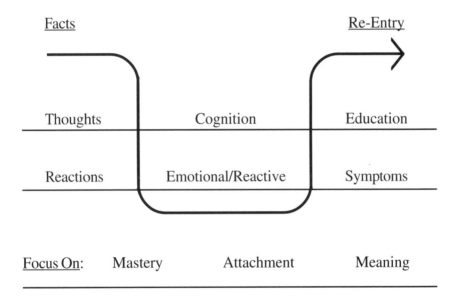

have utilized. Facilities are encouraged to be as creative as possible in the examples that they choose, and to use real examples from the facility, if they are available.

*Individual Crisis Counseling:*
1. A staff member is on the floor and is bleeding from the mouth, after a restraint procedure. A second employee is crying, but otherwise mute.

2.  A patient has a heart attack in the seclusion room, and two mental health workers are immobilized by their fear of this medical crisis.

3.  An employee victim lies on the floor of the day hall with a broken leg, subsequent to a patient assault. As she awaits the ambulance, she is completely abandoned by the staff.

4.  An employee in a restraint procedure was smashed into the wall and died instantly. The body is on the floor in the day hall, while the coroner is en route. Two severely agitated employees pace about the body, and threaten revenge on the patient.

5.  A staff member is assaulted by a patient, who threatens to kill him next time. The employee shrugs and declines ASAP.

*Critical Incident Stress Debriefing:*

1.  A fire occurred in the dormitory area on the unit. No one died, but several staff and patients had smoke inhalation. Five patients refuse to return to the unit.

2.  Multiple assaults were perpetrated by one patient on three staff and two other patients. One nurse has requested a transfer off of the unit. One patient remains in the hospital on the danger list.

3.  A much loved staff member is killed in a car accident on her way to work. Everyone is grief stricken. When the CISD begins,

       the patients ask to place an empty
       chair in the center of the circle for
       their fallen staff member.

4.  After a fifteenth episode of assault
       by one patient in a three week
       period, the patients send a written
       petition to the unit director
       requesting safety and the transfer
       of the violent patient. The clinical
       staff is angry with the
       management over these same
       matters.

*Ongoing Training*

These initial formal trainings are augmented with monthly inservice trainings, which may include guest speakers on topics of relevance to the team's needs as well as role-plays of difficult situations that are actually encountered by team members in the facilities. These latter examples are particularly helpful to the team in improving ASAP service delivery.

On-going trainings include the monthly training for all ASAP team members, the reading of new and relevant published findings, and the attendance by team members at local and national conferences that address violence and trauma. The team leader is responsible for training all new staff, as needed.

ASAP team members are also encouraged to educate others. To date, ASAP members have made conference presentations in six states, have published several journal articles, and have written for professional society newsletters.

This constant exchange of information in a variety of formats is one method of managing the quality of service delivery.

## ASAP DOCUMENTATION

The documents directly utilized in the delivery of ASAP services are shown in figures 17 through 19, and include the four-page ASAP Individual Crisis Intervention Report form, the ASAP Group Services Report Form, a three-page handout given to all employee victims, and the ASAP Release of Information form. The correct use of these forms is explained in detail on the first training day for first line responders.

The four pages of the report form for individual crisis intervention debriefings by ASAP team members is noted in figure 17. Page one includes a brief description of the assault as well as where and when it occurred. A brief note is made of any medical procedures or interventions that were necessary as a result of the assault. The remainder of page one is a detailed account of the employee victim's response to being victimized. Special emphasis is placed on disruptions in mastery, attachment, and meaning as well as the presence of any symptoms associated with psychological trauma and PTSD. Any initial plans to restore the victim's sense of mastery, attachment, and meaning are noted here.

Page two provides for similar narratives of the victim's response three days post-incident, and again at ten days post-incident. As with the original incident, any further or additional disruptions in mastery, attachment, and meaning are noted along with any changes in symptomatology and indicators of recovery.

Page three provides the ASAP team member with specific prompts about common disruptions in mastery, attachment, and meaning as well as a listing of the more common physical, intrusive, and avoidant symptoms of psychological trauma and PTSD. There is a check list of boxes for the first onsite visit as well as for the second (three day) and third (ten day) follow-ups. These prompts were developed to assist ASAP team members onsite, and to increase ASAP team member debriefing reliability. This sheet serves as a helpful summary, when the report form is completed.

Page four documents the characteristics of the assaultive patient. Age, gender, diagnosis, substance abuse, and histories of violence toward others as well as personal victimization are the key areas of inquiry. This information is obtained orally from the staff or by a quick review of the patient's medical record.

The information gathered in this process forms the ASAP record of the event for the employee victim, should the victim request it later on. This is also the basic information that is recorded in the data collection process in figures 10 through 14.

An examination of figure 17A - D and figure 14 will show that the ASAP report form in figure 17 is matched to each of the columns in figure 14, the most advanced of the data collection sheets.

# Figure 17A

## ASAP Individual Report Form - Page 1:

### URBAN HOSPITAL

### ASAP: ASSAULTED STAFF ACTION PROGRAM

SHIFT:_____          TIME:_____

UNIT:_____          DATE:_____

STAFF VICTIM: _____

DESCRIPTION OF ASSAULT:_____

_____

_____

_____

WAS THIS RELATED TO RESTRAINT AND SECLUSION
PROCEDURES:_____

INJURIES/ACTION TAKEN/RESULTS:_____

_____

_____

_____

STAFF VICTIM RESPONSE TO INITIAL ASAP SESSION (Mastery, Attachment,
Meaning): _____

_____

_____

_____

ASAP TEAM MEMBER(S) RESPONDING: _____

_____

TIME OF RESPONSE BY ASAP TEAM MEMBER(S): _____

_____          _____
SIGNATURE                            SIGNATURE

(1)

# Figure 17B

## ASAP Individual Report Form - Page 2:

### URBAN HOSPITAL

### ASAP: ASSAULTED STAFF ACTION PROGRAM

STAFF VICTIM: _____

UNIT: _____

DATE OF ASSAULT: _____

THIRD DAY FOLLOW-UP DATE: _____

RESPONSE (Mastery, Attachment, Meaning): _____

_____
_____
_____
_____
_____
_____
_____

TEN DAY FOLLOW-UP: DATE: _____

RESPONSE (Mastery, Attachment, Meaning): _____

_____
_____
_____
_____
_____
_____
_____

Today's Date: _____

ASAP Team Member: _____

(2)

# Figure 17C

## ASAP Individual Report Form - Page 3:

### URBAN HOSPITAL

### INADEQUATE COPING BY THE VICTIM: ASAP TEAM MEMBERCHECKLIST

| Mastery (Staff Member is): | 1st | 2nd | 3rd |
|---|---|---|---|
| Visibly shaken | | | |
| Chose to leave worksite | | | |
| Is medically injured and must leave worksite | | | |
| Reports feeling overwhelmed and out of control | | | |
| Reports feeling surprised but otherwise fine | | | |
| Dismisses incident and seems in control | | | |
| Needs help but refuses help | | | |
| Uses denial totally | | | |
| Other | | | |
| **Attachments (Staff Member Is):** | | | |
| Unable to turn to other staff | | | |
| Unable to turn to unit managers | | | |
| Is unable to talk to individual supervisor | | | |
| Will not come to staff victim's support group | | | |
| Can not turn to family | | | |
| Does not have adequate support network of any kind | | | |
| Other | | | |
| **Meaning (Staff Member Is):** | | | |
| Not attributing violence to psychosis | | | |
| Not to recent known event in patient's life (e.g., visit by family) | | | |
| Not to changes in the hospital | | | |
| Not to the assault being part of the job | | | |
| Unable to make meaningful sense of what has happened | | | |
| Other | | | |
| **Physical Symptoms:** | | | |
| Hypervigilance | | | |
| Exaggerated startle response | | | |
| Difficulty sleeping | | | |
| Difficulty with concentration or memory | | | |
| Mood irritability - especially anger and depression | | | |
| **Intrusive Symptoms:** | | | |
| Recurring distressing recollections (thoughts, memories, dreams, nightmares, flashbacks) | | | |
| Physical or psychological distress at an event that symbolizes the trauma | | | |
| Grief or survivor guilt | | | |
| **Avoidant Symptoms:** | | | |
| Avoiding specific thoughts, feelings, activities or situations | | | |
| Diminished interest in significant activities | | | |
| Restricted range of emotions (numbness) | | | |

(3)

# Figure 17D

## ASAP Individual Report Form - Page 4:

### URBAN HOSPITAL

### CHARACTERISTICS OF ASSAULTIVE PATIENTS

SEX: _____ Male _____ Female AGE:_____

PRIMARY DIAGNOSIS: _____Schizophrenia
_____Manic Depressive Illness
_____Major Depressive Episode
_____Personality Disorder
Type:_____
_____Substance Abuse Only
_____Organic Brain Dysfunction
_____Other
Specify:_____

HISTORY OF SUBSTANCE ABUSE: _____ Past
_____ Present
_____ Both

HISTORY OF VIOLENCE TOWARD OTHERS:

_____No _____ Yes (if yes, see below)
_____ Physical
_____Sexual
_____Nonverbal
_____Verbal Threat

HISTORY OF PAST VIOLENT ABUSE IN PATIENT'S OWN LIFE:

_____Physical _____Sexual _____Combat _____Street Crime _____Other

SUBSTANCE ABUSE AT TIME OF ASSAULT
(Alcohol, Drugs, Caffeine) : _____ Yes _____ No

(4)

# Figure 17E

## ASAP Group Services Report Form:

### URBAN HOSPITAL

### ASAP: ASSAULTED STAFF ACTION PROGRAM

_____   CISD
_____   Staff Victims' Support Group
_____   Family Outreach

Incident: _____

Date of Incident: _____

Participants: _____

_____

_____

Minutes of Session (Mastery, Attachment, Meaning):

_____
_____
_____
_____
_____
_____
_____
_____
_____
_____

Today's Date: _____

ASAP Team Member: _____

The use of the data collection process in figure 14 follows easily from the ASAP report form for individual debriefings, and will provide the facility with the richest yield of information for making policy decisions for safety and for service delivery.

Figure 17E contains the all purpose report form for ASAP group services. The ASAP team member checks off which type of ASAP service is being rendered, notes the incident and its date, lists the participants in the service rendered, and then records the minutes of the session. Again, the important roles of mastery, attachment, and meaning are emphasized as well as the presence of any symptoms. Possible treatment plans and the course of progress over time are noted in any subsequent meetings that may occur.

Figure 18 lists the four pages of handouts for *all* employee victims, even if they decline ASAP services. The first page presents a brief discussion of traumatic violence and the role of ASAP. This page also includes a listing of all ASAP team members and their hospital telephone extensions. Occasionally, an employee victim will want to utilize the ASAP service, but will feel uncomfortable with the ASAP team member on-call. This may be due to gender, personal issues, political conflicts, professional identity, supervisory responsibility, and the like. In these cases, the employee victim chooses the team member with whom he or she would feel more comfortable. No questions are asked about the substitution that was requested. The ASAP team member onsite contacts the requested ASAP peer, who in turn goes to the site of the assault and debriefs the victim. The first ASAP team member remains on-call for the duration of the day or weekend, as the case may be.

The second page of the handouts for victims includes the possible symptoms of Acute Stress Disorder that may be associated with patient assaults. This information is drawn from the *Diagnostic and Statistical Manual IV* of the American Psychiatric Association (1994). This information is provided to help employee victims understand that their possible responses to these events are understood by the medical community, and may be common outcomes in these kinds of situations.

The next two pages are drawn from information sent to ASAP by a trauma debriefing team at the Detroit Psychiatric Institute. One page outlines several simple strategies for coping with the stress of the assault, in addition to any ASAP services that may be offered.  These basic suggestions cover daily routines, the need to be with others, and the importance of not medicating the post-incident distress with drugs or alcohol.

We know from the published literature (Flannery, 1992, 1994) and from ASAP experience that assaults on employees may significantly impact their families.  Such matters also need to be addressed.  Toward that end, ASAP offers employee victim family counseling; and the fourth page of the employee's handouts also addresses these matters.  It is written for family members and offers basic suggestions on how family members may be of assistance to their loved ones, who have been assaulted.

ASAP routinely gives these employee victim handouts, even when services are refused.  We have found them to be helpful adjuncts to victims who accept ASAP services, and useful reminders to those who decline.  Almost all victims read them and find them useful aids.

This is especially true of those who have initially declined ASAP.  As the impact of the event continues, those who have refused come to realize that they are victims of acute distress and reach out for help, if not immediately, then at some future point or during a subsequent assault.  By reading the handouts, they have learned something about traumatic events and ASAP, and are less inclined to refuse ASAP.  Consider the following examples.

A male mental health worker was victimized by patient assaults several times over a four year period.  Having been a corrections officer earlier in his work career, he repeatedly declined ASAP services by noting that he had to deal with more severe violence in prison settings.  These patient assaults were serious for the most part, and he was told each time that ASAP would be there, should he change his mind.

One day in the fourth year, the employee came to the ASAP team leader.  He was depressed and near tears.  His mother had died, and her loss was reminding him of some of the patient assaults, where he was at a loss to control the situation.

Another example.  A nurse with twenty years of experience sustained a sharp blow to the shoulder by a patient, when she was administering medication to the patient in the seclusion room.  She declined ASAP.  Five weeks later, this same nurse was driving home, and was the first person upon the scene of a bad car accident.  She

# Figure 18A

## ASAP Victim Handouts - Page 1:

**URBAN HOSPITAL**

**ASSAULTED STAFF ACTION PROGRAM (ASAP)**

Dear _____ :

Enclosed is some information that will help you to deal with the trauma.

When human beings are suddenly confronted with situations that are frightening and beyond their control, they can become distressed, apprehensive and feel that things are out of control. Medical research demonstrates that when individuals are able to discuss the event and the feelings it produced at that time, they will cope more effectively with the problem and minimize the risk of long-lasting fears.

We hope that your contact with the A.S.A.P. volunteer was beneficial in helping you to cope with your understandable response to being a victim of an assault. The information that you shared with your A.S.A.P. team member is confidential

Please feel free to contact anyone on the A.S.A.P. team. We would be pleased to assist you.

Sincerely,

ASAP Team Leader

ASAP Team Members                                   Hospital Extension

1. _____

2. _____

3. _____

4. _____

5. _____

# Figure 18B

## ASAP Victim Handout - Page 2:

---

### URBAN HOSPITAL

### ACUTE STRESS DISORDER

### POSSIBLE SYMPTOMS

I.   *Physical Symptoms of Anxiety or Increased Physiological Arousal*

    A.   Hypervigilance

    B.   Difficulty falling or staying asleep

    C.   Exaggerated startle response

    D.   Difficulty concentrating

    E.   Irritability or outbursts of anger

II.  *Intrusive Memories of the Traumatic Event*

    A.   A subjective sense of feeling numb

    B.   Absence of emotional responsiveness

    C.   Reduced awareness of surroundings

    D.   Depersonalization

    E.   Dissociative amnesia

    F.   Intrusive recollections (e.g., memories, daydreams, nightmares)

III. *Avoidance of Events that May Arouse Recollections of the Trauma*

# Figure 18C

## ASAP Victim Handouts - Page 3:

### URBAN HOSPITAL

### STRESS MANAGEMENT AND COPING STRATEGIES AFTER TRAUMATIC EVENTS

1. Acknowledge your emotions as a *NORMAL* reaction to an *ABNORMAL* situation.

2. Express your thoughts and feelings about the event as often as necessary. Find people who are good listeners and talk to them. Talking helps reduce the intensity of feelings, helps you feel more in control, helps you identify what you feel, and clarifies issues in your mind.

3. Work towards accepting the traumatic event and its consequences.

4. Keep your daily life as normal as possible.

5. Spend time with others who are supportive.

6. Do things that feel good and increase feelings of self-control.

7. Find time to relax, exercise, and eat properly (avoid nicotine and caffeine).

8. Structure your time — keep busy.

9. Avoid using unprescribed drugs or alcohol as a method of coping with stress.

10. Don't be frightened by traumatic stress reaction.

11. Don't take what happened personally. "Why did this happen to me? What did I do to deserve this?"

12. Deal with feelings of guilt. Don't take responsibility for what happened. Realize that you cannot always control what is happening around you. You can, however, control your response to the situation. Don't take responsibility for events beyond your control.

13. Cope with fear and vulnerability. Realize that fear and feeling vulnerable come from the perception of danger and not from weakness.

14. Avoid comparing yourself with others. Each person will react in his/her own way.

15. Talk to family members about the event so you all can share a supportive view.

16. Give yourself appropriate time to work through a critical incident. (Normally six to eight weeks.)

17. Seek peer or professional counseling, if necessary.

# Figure 18D

## ASAP Victim Handouts - Page 4:

---

### URBAN HOSPITAL

### TRAUMATIC INCIDENT STRESS INFORMATION FOR FAMILIES

Your loved one has been involved in an emotion-charged event, often knownas atraumatic incident. He/she may be experiencing *NORMAL* stress responses to such an event, which are traumatic incident stress responses.

Traumatic incident stress affects over 80% of all workers exposed to a critical incident in line of duty. No one in this type of work is immune to traumatic incident stress, regardless of past experience or years of service.

The following are important things to remember about traumatic incident stress:

1. The signs of traumatic incident stress are physical, cognitive (thoughts), emotional (feelings) and behavioral. Your loved one has received a handout outlining these signs. Please ask him/her to share it with you.

2. Traumatic incident stress response can occur right away at the scene, or within hours, days, or even within weeks, after the event.

3. Your loved one may experience a variety of signs/symptoms of a stress response or he/she may not feel any of the signs at this time. It depends on the individual.

4. Suffering from the effects of traumatic incident stress is completely normal. Your loved one is not the only one suffering — co-workers shared the event, and are probably having the same or similar reactions.

5. The symptoms will normally subside and disappear in time, if you and your loved one do not dwell upon them and allow yourselves the chance to deal with what has taken place.

6. Encourage, but do not pressure, your loved one to talk about the incident and his her reactions to it. Talk is the best medicine. Your primary "job" is to listen and reassure. Remember that, if an event is upsetting to you and your loved one, your children may be affected too. They may need to talk also.

7. You may not understand what your loved one is going through at this time, but you can offer your love and support. Don't be afraid to ask what you can do that he/she would consider helpful. Also try not to feel offended if he/she withdraws from the family or becomes overly protective. These are normal reactions to the event.

8. Accept the fact that life will go on. Maintain or return to a normal routine as soon as possible and maintain a health life-style. Exercise, rest, and eating well balanced meals are important.

9. If the signs of stress your loved one is experiencing do not begin to subside within a few weeks, or, if they intensify, consider seeking further assistance.

---

 successfully administered cardiopulmonary resuscitation to one of the victims. When she stood up, she was shaking, and called the ASAP team leader from a pay telephone by the roadside.

The nonverbal presence of an ASAP program with its process of continuing education and gentle outreach, even when refused, creates a sense of community.

Figure 19 is the ASAP release of information form, an important component in assuring confidentiality. Any employee victim can request his or her ASAP record(s) for medical or insurance reasons, and that request is handled thoughtfully. The ASAP team leader, the ASAP team member who responded to the incident (if possible), and the employee meet to review the record. The employee can ask any questions for purposes of clarification, and then signs the release. The ASAP team leader then mails the ASAP report to the intended recipient. This process not only assures the employee victim of confidentiality, but serves as a symbolic reminder to the rest of the hospital community that ASAP communications are kept in confidence.

Figure 20 is the last document directly related to the training day. It is the ASAP graduation certificate that inducts the trainee into the ASAP program. It is a highly prized document that is frequently displayed on office walls.

## AN ASAP TEAM: THE EXPERIENCE OF ITS MEMBERS

Having described the ASAP approach to violence and how to field such a program, it is reasonable to ask what its members think of their ASAP experiences.

In those ASAP programs that are successfully fielded and managed by a strong ASAP team leader, there is usually a strong sense of mission, of service to others in need. People are drawn to health care, in part, because of their concern for others, and this concern includes their assaulted colleagues. Patient assaults on staff are a pervasive problem (Blair, 1991; Davis, 1991), and the need is great. ASAP members bond strongly, and form a cohesive unit that has a strong sense of responsibility for the psychological welfare of the workforce. Often, there are waiting lists to join the team, and it is rare for a team member to resign, unless the employee is being transferred or is retiring.

# Figure 19

## ASAP Release of Information Form:

**URBAN HOSPITAL**

**ASAP RELEASE OF INFORMATION FORM**

To:      Director, Assaulted Staff Action Program

I,_____ , formally
request that a copy of my ASAP records, completed by ASAP
Team member,_____
for my assault on ____*(date)*____ , be forwarded to:

(Name, address)

I verify that I have reviewed my ASAP record with the ASAP
team leader, and understand fully what has been written about
my assault and my response to it.

_____
*(Name Printed in Full)*

_____
*(Signature)*

_____
*(Today's Date)*

# Figure 20

**ASAP Graduation Certificate:**

---

## URBAN HOSPITAL

## THE ASSAULTED STAFF ACTION PROGRAM (ASAP)

### Graduation Certificate

We hereby acknowledge that

_____ (name) _____

on this _____ day of, 19 __
has successfully completed the
necessary training to become
an ASAP team member.

_____          _____
Chief Operating Officer                          ASAP Team Leader

---

Professional development is another common theme among team members. Many develop strong interests in psychological trauma and emergency services. Some seek additional formal training beyond ASAP, and develop these skills as components of their professional practice. Not surprisingly, some have gone on to join additional community crisis response teams in their non-work related hours. Others have added trauma counseling to the private practice services that they offer.

A third theme invokes an attempt to address the cultural resistance to victimization. As ASAP team members learn about psychological trauma and its pervasiveness, they are also confronted by resistance to acknowledging the plight of their own colleague victims in their own facility by their own fellow workers. Seeing health care providers minimize the importance of psychological trauma serves as an impetus for many in ASAP to focus their efforts on de-stigmatizing victims of violence both in the hospital and in society at large.

Perhaps, the most telling indicator of the experience of being an ASAP team member is that ASAP team members seek to extend their ASAP service by establishing ASAP teams at subsequent postings, and persuading their colleagues in other facilities to do the same.

## STANDARDS OF PERFORMANCE AND CLINICAL PRACTICE GUIDELINES

For an ASAP team to operate effectively, there must be clear Standards of Performance and Clinical Practice Guidelines that shape the quality and cost-effectiveness of the ASAP service delivery system.

Standards of Performance state what is to be done and within what time frame. Clinical Practice Guidelines provide the information on how these services should be rendered. Tables 1 and 2 outline the standards and guidelines for all ASAP programs.

# Table 1

## ASAP Standards of Performance:

1.  All services are provided promptly, courteously, and with compassion.

2.  Confidentiality is strictly adhered to except in those rare cases where the employee victim reports committing a crime. In these cases, team members are to follow any mandated reporting requirements.

3.  Services are rendered by those with the necessary, established training and expertise for any given service.

4.  Services are sensitive to cultural and linguistic differences, where possible.

5.  Teams respond to all four types of patient assaults (physical, sexual, nonverbal intimidation, verbal threat). A system is developed to triage which assaults are to be addressed. This triage is based on staffing requirements and starts with physical assaults.

6.  Individual Crisis Debriefings occur on-site and within fifteen minutes to one hour, if the team member is on duty. If off-shift hours, the team member speaks with the unit and the employee victim to assess need.

7.  The three- and ten-day individual follow-up debriefings are completed by the same team member who did the original debriefings.

8.  All employee victims receive the psychological trauma informational handouts with the basic information provided by victims' assistant programs. These handouts are given to those who decline services.

# Table 1

## ASAP Standards of Performance (continued):

9. Critical Incident Stress Debriefing (CISD) interventions occur on-site, preferably within one week. CISD debriefings are always co-led by the team leader and/or team supervisors. The team leader conducts the CISD, whenever possible.

10. The Staff Victims' Support Group occurs weekly, on-site, and overlaps two shifts. It is co-led by the team leader and one supervisor. During periods of staffing shortage, the team leader may meet with staff victims individually at mutually convenient times.

11. Family debriefings, when requested, are conducted by a team member who is a specialist in family counseling.

12. Professional Referrals to outside trauma specialists shall be made within four weeks, if clinically feasible.

13. Written formal agreements are required for services to be provided to other agencies.

14. The team leader is responsible for:

    A. Obtaining necessary Informed Consent for data collection, when the program begins and when new hires start.

    B. Securing all ASAP records in a locked and safe area.

    C. Deciding if the team will respond to other types of traumatic events in the facility beyond assaults.

    D. Monitoring team members for possible vicarious traumatization.

    E. All data collection procedures.

    F. Training all new ASAP team members as needed.

# Table 2

## ASAP Clinical Practice Guidelines:

1. All interventions restore or foster the skills of Stress-Resistant Persons (Flannery, 1990, 1994), especially in the domains of mastery, attachment, and meaning.

2. Individual crisis debriefings follow accepted clinical guidelines (Sandoval, 1985), and emphasize immediacy of need, the victim's feelings, acknowledgement of the crisis, focused problem-solving, and victim self-reliance.

3. CISD debriefings will follow accepted protocols (Mitchell & Everly, 1996), and include the facts, thoughts, reactions/feelings, symptoms, and coping strategies for each incident.

4. The Staff Victims' Support Group adheres to the basic principles of group dynamics (Yalom, 1970).

5. Family debriefings adhere to the basic principles of family counseling (American Psychiatric Association, 1984)

This completes our review of the steps necessary to ensure the successful fielding of an ASAP team. When the team is trained, the service is fielded, and its benefits for the facility can begin.

Life, politics, and social systems being what they are, not all ASAP teams are fielded smoothly. There are problems. Perhaps surprisingly, the problems from agency to agency are fairly similar and, in their own way, parallel the five steps needed to field a team in the first place.

The next chapter focuses on these common problems, and presents the solutions that have been effective thus far. As we noted earlier, no ASAP team is successfully fielded without administrative support, and we start our inquiry of the commonly encountered issues there.

# chapter

# 5

## ASAP: COMMON ISSUES

*Hello darkness, my old friend.*
                            - Paul Simon

*There is a destiny that makes us brothers,*
*None goes his way alone.*
                            - Oliver Wendell Holmes

Forty-five-year-old Wally was a shy man. He had been that way since he was fifteen.

A confirmed bachelor, in his off-duty hours he volunteered at a shelter for homeless families, and looked after the needs of the children that he had never had. Down on their luck due to fire, poverty, domestic battering, parental drug abuse and the like, these children were continuously depressed. He helped with their needs at the shelter, and took them for weekly visits to the local fast food restaurant. Burgers and fries occasionally cheered even the most saddened child.

The call was struck at 12:17 A.M. Wally jumped from bed, dragged on his work clothes, slid down the pole, and climbed into the driver's seat. Every minute meant life. As the doors opened, with lights flashing, pumper Engine 71 pulled out into the darkness.

Fire fully engulfed the rear of the one-story, framed fast-food restaurant. As Wally and his fellow firefighters entered from the front, they smelled kerosene. Their search for possible occupants was impaired by thick, heavy smoke. Wally stumbled across two bodies. He recognized them instantly from his weekend visits. One was the manager, Mr. Halpern. The other was Susan, a sixteen-year-old high school student, who worked the counter part-time to earn money for college. Both had been shot several times in the head.

Six hours later back at the station, Wally wrestled with sleeplessness. Always quiet, he was now completely withdrawn into himself. Life is a gift. Firemen are trained to save lives. Any time. Any one. Anywhere. The call is answered. Losing life to a fire is difficult for any firefighter, but what does one say in the face of the murder of two neighbors?

Within forty-eight hours, the police had determined that a recently fired employee of the restaurant had returned at the close of business, shot Mr. Halpern and Susan to death, robbed the cash register, and then attempted to cover-up the crime by setting the building on fire.

After his shift, Wally took a drink to steady his nerves. He thought back thirty years earlier when his father, also a firefighter, had come home, and was close to tears. His father had watched five people burn to death as he attempted in vain to reach them. Wally was fifteen, and family life had never been quite the same after this happened.

What would he say to the children at the shelter?

Here is another example of the possible multiple impacts of a violent act for which an ASAP program could be of assistance. Victims here include the family members of those who were murdered, the other employees of the restaurant, the firefighters, and possibly the children from the shelter. Each group must deal in its own way with two crimes perpetrated by the disgruntled employee: murder and arson. While there may be support groups for the families and colleagues, how will the needs of the firefighters and their families be addressed? They were, after all, witnesses to the arson, and were the first on the scene of the crime on the restaurant floor. We know for at least one firefighter this present loss of life has served as a trigger for memories of a past painful fire that victimized his entire family, even though only his father was actually present at the fire itself. Again, ASAP programs can be designed to be at the ready in times such as these. Debriefing now may minimize the possibility of a long term negative impact such as that experienced by Wally and his family several years ago.

While the fielding of an ASAP program can be outlined in

clear, logical steps, the world itself is more complex. Issues and problems in fielding an ASAP team can and do arise, and need to be addressed. This process of monitoring services and improving their effectiveness is known as quality management (Walton, 1986). Quality management seeks to continuously improve what is currently being done and to incorporate new advances in knowledge so that the quality of services is the best that it can be and is provided in a cost-effective manner. Each ASAP program should have its own quality management process so that any ASAP team that is fielded, such as one for the firefighters and their families in the present case, can assure the victims that their psychological needs are being fully and skillfully addressed. Victims deserve nothing less.

In this chapter we shall examine the basic and most common issues that have been encountered by ASAP programs since their beginning in 1990 (Flannery, 1988). To assist the reader in utilizing the materials presented in this chapter, they have been arranged in the same sequence of steps as in chapter three: 1.) administration, 2.) design, 3.) selection, 4.) training, and 5.) fielding the team. In this way, the reader can cross reference each step with the tasks that need to be successfully addressed (chapter three), with some of the problems most likely to be encountered (present chapter).

We noted as we began chapter three that administrative support was crucial for the success of an ASAP team. The reverse is also true. Lack of administrative support creates fundamental problems in fielding an ASAP team, and we begin our short review of common problems there.

## 1. ADMINISTRATIVE SUPPORT

The administrative problems encountered by the ASAP programs have fallen into three categories: lack of administrative support, the impact of managed care initiatives, and negative managerial attitudes.

### General Issues

The lack of administrative support is a serious roadblock to the efficient functioning of an ASAP team. That lack of support can take one of several common shapes. First is the problem of lack of support from the start. In these cases, a senior manager does not really want an ASAP team, but is required to have one because of the decision of a more senior manager. The senior manager immediately responsible for the team will delay its design, impede the selection of team members, fail to free the staff for training, not allow the team the use of the inhouse mails to announce the start of the program, not mandate the reporting of assaults, etc. ASAP has encountered all of these maneuvers to undercut a team's functioning, and it is an exceedingly difficult problem for the facility's ASAP team leader. Senior managers commonly adopt this stance because they believe that violence comes with the turf, because they themselves may be victims of untreated PTSD, or because they believe that ASAP pampers employees.

A second form of lack of administrative support comes about because of administrative personnel changes. In these cases, the first senior manager who strongly supported ASAP resigns or is reassigned, and the replacement has differing priorities, which do not include support of the ASAP program. These administrators usually are not against ASAP, but they do not wish to expend political capital on the team and its work.

A third common form of lack of administrative support relates to a political struggle within the agency in which the ASAP program becomes a pawn. For example, senior management authorizes an ASAP team, but the middle managers block employee victims from utilizing its services because they are angry with management about the number of violent patients in the system or inadequate procedures for restraint. The focus is on ASAP, but the real issues lie elsewhere.

We have not found very good solutions to the lack of administrative support. Obvious strategies include pressing ahead anyway as best one can, building other inhouse coalitions for support, and waiting out the manager, until the changing health care system results in a new management team. We do know that support of the ASAP team leader by other ASAP personnel is crucial in biding one's time.

Managed care is a second disruptive administrative issue. The health care system is undergoing a dramatic period of change nationally with several new initiatives being undertaken. These repeated changes impact the social systems of the facilities.

To begin with, there is now a constant tension between community-based and hospital-based programs, as many services are re-located and privatized in the community. For hospitals, this may mean facilities are downsized and employees are laid off. It may also include budget cuts, decreases in overtime, salaried blocks not being filled, staffing shortages that cause reassignments which result in employee displacements from their patients and units, extra assignments on the shift, and no established days off.

The situation in the community may be equally strained. Difficult patients are now being discharged to community placements, but, in general, the community staff are younger, less formally educated, and less experienced. In addition, in many settings these staff do not have the tools needed for adequate patient restraint and seclusion nor the necessary number of colleagues to make a show of force. Having to call the emergency room or wait for the police is of limited assistance. This is further compounded by fewer and shorter admissions. Underfunding of many community programs may preclude additional staffing and further training in the clinical skills necessary for managing aggressive patients. In addition, many community residences have older male patients cared for by younger female staff, and an unacceptable increase in the number of sexual assaults by these patients on staff have been documented (Flannery et al., 1994).

In these circumstances, staff may be physically at work but actively avoiding patient contact. Patients may respond with anger and assaultive behavior. Similarly, fewer staff may lead to increased staff fear. This often results in more limit setting. Patients then feel abandoned, and strike out at the caregivers.

Managers confronted with these initiatives, where the rules keep changing, have a difficult task to manage. Some general rules of thumb have proven helpful. The first is to keep open lines of communication to minimize rumors and unnecessary anxiety; the second is to minimize the disruption of services as much as is possible so that mastery and attachments are sustained; and the third is to provide discussion groups for staff to present concerns and grievances, if need be. ASAP team leaders have worked with managers in these difficult times to establish the minimum staffing needed for the ASAP program in ways that do not further complicate the larger staffing shortages.

A final, general administrative issue has been that of the negative attitudes of some managers. As we have seen, these have included the stance that violence is part of the job, that ASAP coddles staff or interferes with the clinical work, that psychological trauma is not a real medical problem, or that the facility cannot afford the time or manpower for an ASAP program. We have seen staff victims intimidated into rejecting ASAP services on more than one occasion.

These attitudes reflect the attitudes of many in the culture at large about psychological trauma. We have chosen to deal with these attitudes through education, and by letting the results of ASAP speak for themselves. This approach has proven effective in many, but not all, cases.

### Legal Issues

In general, we have not found the legal issues to be problematic. Facilities that have adhered to the guidelines noted earlier for Informed Consent, joint facility agreements, malpractice insurance, and so forth have continued unimpeded in their efforts to provide ASAP services.

### Financial Matters

Here again, ASAP has not encountered difficulties in the fiscal area. When fiscal issues have arisen (e.g., no money is provided for beepers), these issues are more a function of lack of administrative support than true dollar-cost issues.

### 2. DESIGNING THE TEAM

If the steps for designing the team were followed correctly as the program started, there should be no basic design flaws at a later date. However, ASAP has found two ancillary issues that are worth noting.

The first concerns large service systems with several patient-care sites. Frequently, these facilities want ASAP services, but are not willing to contribute team members. A similar situation may result if a team has a request to expand into a second or different service system. In both cases, the new sites may plead staffing shortages as their reasons for not contributing team members.

Since ASAP seeks to create community, we have not included those patient-care sites that are not willing to be equal and active participants. Some have then joined; others have remained intransigent in their views.

# 3. SELECTING THE TEAM

## Team Leaders

Being an ASAP team leader is a challenging task that requires true dedication. ASAP team leaders have proven less than effective when they do not "own" the team, and do not have enthusiasm for the task. This is further complicated if they are generally passive, feel overwhelmed and angered by the changes in the system, and do not think managerially. The disinterest on the part of the leader permeates throughout the team, and a helpful solution for this problem is to add a team co-leader so that responsibilities are shared.

We have found that team leaders need to be cheerleaders in these difficult times in health care. They need to exhort their members, enter various competitions to showcase their team, and provide an annual anniversary party on the start date of ASAP. Team members volunteer thousands of hours of service, and receive little recognition, and team leaders can be helpful in this regard in sustaining morale.

Replacing team leaders has been an unanticipated problem. As team leaders have retired in the midst of the current staffing shortages, it has proven difficult to influence the choice of replacements. Interested ASAP team members may not be able to be released from their current responsibilities to become the team leader. ASAP has chosen to meet with the managers, to explain the necessary characteristics for ASAP team leadership, and to work with the managers to resolve the issue within the very real limitations faced by the managers. We have not been able to fully groom our own replacements as we would prefer to do.

## Team Members

Two matters pertaining to team members have occurred. The first is an enormous staff turnover of staff in many community-based agencies. This is disruptive to ASAP services, disruptive to team cohesion, and requires almost constant training of new hires by the team leader. One solution to this problem has been to select the house managers or program directors as ASAP team members, because the turnover in these positions is considerably less than that of line staff.

We have discussed the second issue earlier, but it is important and bears repeating because it results in unnecessary suffering. It involves ASAP team members who are also victims of untreated PTSD. The work of ASAP precipitates intrusive memories in some, and their effectiveness as team members is impaired. An ASAP team is not a process for the vicarious treatment of a past history of victimization. This matter of past, personal victimization should be addressed in a general way when selecting new team members, and team leaders need to monitor all team members in this regard. Victims are always welcomed as team members, when their personal issues have been adequately addressed.

### Team Supplies

The securing of team supplies has not been a problem unless a manager has been withholding supplies as a way of impeding the team.

### 4. TRAINING THE TEAM

Training the team has not been so much of the problem as providing ongoing training to keep skills sharpened and finely honed. Most ASAP programs have been impacted by staffing shortages in their facilities. This has meant cutbacks in inservice training time. When assaults are infrequent, some ASAP team members may become unsure of their debriefing skills.

ASAP has developed several possible approaches to this problem. One is to have smaller teams. In this way, members are on-call for longer periods of time, but their chances of being called to do an ASAP debriefing are substantially increased. Another approach is to send ASAP members in teams of two so that no one team member needs to be concerned about overlooking some important aspect of the debriefing. (Team leaders can provide this same service by reviewing debriefing procedures before a single ASAP member does a debriefing.)

Other approaches to maintain skill level have included doing mock ASAP debriefings, when the hospital stages mock medical emergencies; interviewing patients who are restrained and secluded to learn why these patients were assaultive; interviewing employee witnesses of violence, and providing debriefing procedures for the security force of the facility. This latter group may have important

# Table 1

## ASAP: Employee Victim Injury Code:

1. Soft Tissue Bruise with or without swelling
2. Head or Back Injury
3. Bone/Tendon/Ligament Injury
4. Open Wound/Scratches/Spitting
5. Abdominal Trauma
6. Psychological Fright/No Tissue Injury

concerns subsequent to witnessing the violence, and staffing limitations do not always permit an adequate assessment of these employees' needs.

ASAP teams also need to develop better training procedures in two domains. First, ASAP team members need better methods for determining disruptions in mastery, attachment, and meaning so that the subjective response of the employee victim is adequately recorded. Asking employee victims about what was helpful and what could be helpful in gathering information in the debriefing process are important first steps. Secondly, the ASAP injury list in table 1 needs further refinement. Currently, team members record the most serious injury in each incident, but sometimes there are multiple injuries, and this data is not recorded systematically at present. Equally important is the current absence of method of rating the severity of the injury. Here we need to develop some system that rates severity both by the employee victim as well as the ASAP team member. ASAP members will then need to be trained in these procedures to ensure reliability.

## 5. FIELDING THE TEAM

The most common problems encountered in fielding the team are failures in mandated reporting, in not observing the changing nature of the patients prone to be assaultive, and in the lack of continuing education for the general workforce about psychological trauma.

Underreporting by managerial staff can arise from the beliefs that violence is part of the job or that assaults are not serious problems in most cases. On occasion, it is motivated politically to preclude a true understanding of the extent of violence on a unit. In these circumstances, ASAP team leaders need to work continuously with senior management until an accurate reporting system is in place, and employee victims are free from intimidation, if they choose to use ASAP services.

As the nature of health care delivery is changing, so are the characteristics of the patients treated at different sites and the types of problems that these patients are presenting. In the next chapter, we shall present some findings from the ASAP program that specifically relate to this matter and that reveal a dramatic change in the characteristics of the patients now likely to be assaultive. The fielding of any ASAP team requires on-going monitoring of possible sources of violence and the best strategies for ASAP debriefing, when these events occur.

Finally, confronting the impact of violence in our culture is a continuing need. Even in facilities with ASAP programs where violence has declined, employees can be lulled into a false sense of security. Employees may not want the burden of being debriefed, and underreporting may commence. We have seen this happen in facilities with ASAP programs with corresponding subsequent increases in assaults. ASAP team leaders need to persist in their monthly memos to staff to increase, and, then, maintain awareness of the painful negative impact of untreated psychological trauma and PTSD.

This chapter has been brief, but it is important because of its emphasis on quality management as a tool to maintain the highest quality of service that an ASAP team can provide. Table 2 presents a checklist of the more commonly encountered issues.

In the final chapter, we continue our emphasis on the importance of quality management by focusing on the critical role of research in gathering information to improve services. Many have prematurely concluded that, since violence is unpredictable, measuring its impact in controlled, rigorous research designs is all but precluded. This need not necessarily be the case, and in the next chapter we shall explore the methodological issues in general, and the research findings from the ASAP program in particular.

# Table 2

## ASAP: Common Problems Checklist:

[ ] *Administrative Support*
    [ ] Lack of Managerial Support
    [ ] Impact of Managed Care Initiatives
    [ ] Negative Managerial Attitudes

[ ] *Designing the Team*
    [ ] Site Unwillingness to Participate

[ ] *Selecting the Team*
    [ ] Inadequate Team Leader
    [ ] Providing Team Support
    [ ] Replacing Team Leader
    [ ] Line Staff Turnover
    [ ] Line Staff Victims of Past Personal Violence

[ ] *Training the Team*
    [ ] Maintaining Skill Level
    [ ] Better Assessment Measures

[ ] *Fielding the Team*
    [ ] Underreporting
    [ ] Changes in Patient Population
    [ ] Continuing Education

# chapter

# 6

## ASAP: RESEARCH IMPLICATIONS AND FINDINGS

*These pitiful days will come to an end.*
- Anne Frank

*But I have promises to keep*
*And miles to go before I sleep.*
- Robert Frost

This is America.

He had waited a long time to be able to make that statement. His name had been on the immigration waiting list for eleven long years, but he had waited patiently and had practiced his English every day.

Now he was here. It was true that the streets were not paved with gold, but he welcomed freedom and opportunity. He was not adverse to hard work and his job as a driver for Veterans Taxi was his beginning.

He worked two shifts each day, and lived in one room in a single-occupancy apartment. No movies. No restaurants. No sporting events. His church and his fellow drivers were his social outlets. Cerno was a man with a mission, and that mission was to bring his wife and two young daughters to the New World. His long work hours dulled the ache of their absence.

Life in the streets was difficult for taxi drivers. Heavy traffic. Deadbeat fares. Poor tips. Increased costs for fuel and repairs. Nevertheless, for Cerno this was the beginning of his family's future, and he committed the city's streets to memory, as he drove about them each day.

He was hailed in the downtown area by a young male in his

early twenties, who directed Cerno to 138 G Street on the city's northwest side.  The passenger sat sullenly in the back seat, and his breathing was somewhat labored.

Cerno felt uneasy with the broken street lights, abandoned cars, and dilapidated housing in the northwest area, and he quickly located 138 G Street.  What happened next remained unclear — even two days later.

The sullen youth held a knife to Cerno's neck and demanded money.  The assailant then beat Cerno senseless with a plumber's wrench, and left him to die in a pool of blood.  Cerno awoke to severe pain and several tubes in his nose, throat, and arms in the Intensive Care Unit of Harrison General Hospital.

An urban neighbor on the third floor of a nearby dwelling had seen violence like this thrice before, and had called the police.  The neighbor knew what the police had long suspected.  This attempted murder was an initiation rite for membership in a local gang.

This is America?


Here again is an example of violence in America in the late Twentieth Century.  Taxi driving is the most dangerous occupation in the country with a homicide rate forty times greater than any other type of employment.  Serving the public, carrying money, and working alone substantially increase the risk of violence, and taxi drivers face all three of these risk factors.

Here, again, is the type of assailant whose numbers are growing so quickly.  Young men and women between the ages of fifteen and twenty-four, who are long on drugs, alcohol, and weapons; and short on family, education, and hope.  Here, again, are victims in an industry that could greatly benefit from an ASAP team for its workforce.

Such teams, wherever they are found, must not only provide state-of-the-art crisis intervention services, but must also be closely monitoring themselves continually to incorporate advances in treatment and to monitor the quality of their activities.  ASAP teams must be ever vigilant for improvement.  Each ASAP program is guided by the basic principle in medicine and health care: Do no harm.  In this last chapter, we examine the importance of research and quality management in ASAP programs and in Critical Incident Stress Management (CISM) approaches in general.

CISM was developed to meet the needs of emergency services personnel, as we have noted.  After these programs were in place, some studies began to report that CISM approaches were not helpful to all participants in all circumstances (Kenardy, Webster, Lewin, Carr, Hazell, & Carter, 1996).  No intervention in medicine and health science benefits everyone, nor is without side effects in some.  However, this led the parent society of CISM, the International Critical Incident Stress Foundation, to place an even greater emphasis on research.

The early CISD and CISM interventions addressed the needs of emergency services personnel responding to natural and man-made disasters, such as the immediate aftermath of hurricanes, tornadoes, and plane crashes, and to other smaller events.  They did not lend themselves easily to traditional experimental control and measurement.

The ASAP programs, however, were conducted in circumscribed social systems where violence was a frequently expected outcome, and, thus, ASAP was able to conduct needed experimental inquiry from its inception.  Since research is itself a form of ASAP's quality management program for providing more refined services, we shall begin with the research approaches and findings that may prove of assistance for evaluating other CISM approaches.  The chapter then continues with a more general discussion of the role of quality management, and closes with some final thoughts about ASAP.

## ASAP: RESEARCH DESIGN

Designing an adequate research paradigm to measure the effects of CISM approaches is difficult, but not impossible.  Such research will need to include adequate experimental design, good operational definitions, clear outcome measures, and detailed procedures.  Several settings, such as health care settings, are relatively contained social systems where violence is expected and where such research rigor can be developed.  These include schools, colleges, corrections, and probation, among others.  These settings provide specific types of violent critical incidents by a specific group of assailants, and can be studied relatively easily.  These settings also readily lend themselves to assessing the nature and response of employee victims in these various settings.

## Experimental Design

Creating an adequate control group to assess the impact of a CISM intervention is an important component for adequate research, and can be accomplished in several ways. One traditional approach would be to compare a group of victims who received the intervention with another group that received the intervention at a later point in time because of personnel or staffing limitations, or one that did not receive the intervention at all. In this case, the outcome measures of the treatment group could be compared with the same outcome measures of the later group before it receives the treatment, or with the group that received no intervention at all.

Another possible approach is the multiple-baseline design (Hersen & Barlow, 1976) that ASAP utilizes. Here, each hospital serves as its own control group and comes on-line at spaced intervals. This research design requires that all other factors in the hospital remain constant. When this is accomplished, the ASAP program is introduced into each facility at the noted interval. If the outcome measures provide similar results in each of the facilities, then it may be inferred that ASAP is impacting the system.

In cases of natural or man-made disasters, technology now permits the assessment of emergency services personnel needs on-site, the efficacy of CISM approaches on-site, and the impact of these events on the workforce over time. CISM teams could be trained to carry simple measures into the field, such as the Impact of Life Events Scale (Horowitz, Wilner, & Alvarez, 1979). These could be administered quickly and with minimum disruptions in the field immediately prior to CISM interventions, and as workers leave the site. While not as rigorous as the first two approaches noted here, these preliminary approaches would lead to more sophisticated designs at a future date. Several CISM teams employing the same rudimentary design would yield important nationwide, indeed worldwide data, in a few short years.

CISM research design is in its early stages. Systematic efforts will result over time in experimental designs that include repeated measures analyses, multifactorial designs, and advanced multivariate analysis (Winer, 1962).

**Operational Definitions**

The lack of clear and consistent operational definitions of the types of violence being studied, and the types of CISM interventions being employed is a serious and ongoing shortcoming in this area of research.

The published literature on patient assaults on staff in health care settings is fairly extensive, yet even here, after twenty-five years, there is little consistency. Differing studies use differing definitions of physical assault (Blair, 1991; Davis, 1991; Hanson & Balk, 1992; Hunter & Carmel, 1992; Reid, Bollinger, & Edwards, 1989). Some add sexual assault (Dietz & Rada, 1982), and no studies other than those of ASAP (Flannery et al., 1995) appear to have systematically included threats, which are frequent occurrences and often frighten staff.

Opportunities exist in educational, correctional, and health care settings to provide clear definitions of violence, clear definitions of the characteristics of the assailants, and clear definitions of what treatment interventions were employed and how they were implemented.

Operational definitions are also needed for the types of injuries sustained and the severity of those injuries. Variables such as the nature and extent of the injury and the victim's perception of the event should be routinely recorded (Morrison, 1989), and the problem of underreporting (Lion et al., 1981) may need special attention in some settings.

Simple steps in these areas will yield important benefits in our ability to understand and respond to violence and trauma.

**Outcome Measures**

Outcome measures allow us to assess both the impact of the violence and the effectiveness of CISM interventions. Outcome measures can include objective, behavioral indices as well as subjective self-report measures.

Objective, behavioral indicators could include measures such as use of sick leave, medical visits related to the critical incident, Industrial Accident Claims, requests for transfer, staff turnover, and measures of lost productivity.

Subjective, self-report dependent measures could include victim self-ratings of PTSD symptoms as well as disruptions in the domains of mastery, attachment and meaning. There are also a number of formal measures of subjective response that could be fielded. Some of the more common include the Impact of Events Scale (IES; Horowitz, Vilner, & Alvarez, 1979), the Traumatic Stress Schedule (Norris, 1990), and the Potential Stressors Experiences Inventory (Falsetti, Resnick, Kilpatrick, & Freedy, 1994).

**Procedures**

Good experimental research depends on creating studies that can be replicated by other scientists. Clear operational definitions of terms, distinct outcome measures, and fundamental designs will prove of little assistance, if the procedure of how subjects were selected, how and when they were assessed, and how any intervention procedures were implemented are not clearly specified. It is important to note whether the intervention procedure was taught and fielded as originally described, or whether any modifications were added. Any modifications need to be clearly described so that other researchers could follow the same process. Training in procedures should be standardized as much as possible to ensure that observed outcomes are not due to variations in interventions that render the outcome data of limited usefulness.

With these general observations in mind, let us examine the several findings of the ASAP program as one example of the importance of research findings for the development of informed service delivery.

## ASAP: THE FINDINGS

The ASAP findings reported here are in two groupings. The first set of data apply to the original ASAP program in the first state hospital, and are referred to as ASAP I. The second set of data apply to the next three ASAP programs in three additional state hospitals, and are known as ASAP II. Data currently being gathered on the expanded ten-site ASAP program will be reported in future papers in the medical and scientific journals.

The findings from both sets of data are presented in terms of clinical outcomes, declines in assaults, dollar-cost savings, special outcomes, and the changing demographics of assaultive psychiatric inpatients.  The findings from ASAP I include responses to all four types of patient assaults with all ASAP services.  Because of downsizing, privatization, and layoffs in the midst of a severe state fiscal crisis, the ASAP II data include responses to physical and sexual assaults only and with only three of the basic ASAP services: individual crisis intervention, CISD for ward units, and informally conducted staff victims' support groups.  Since these scientific findings have been reported in detail previously (Flannery et al., 1991; Flannery et al., 1995; Flannery et al., 1996; Flannery et al., 1997), only the major findings are highlighted here.

**Clinical Outcomes**

*Employee Victims Who Participated.  ASAP I.*  ASAP I responded to 327 episodes of assault from April, 1990 to January, 1992, when this facility was closed due to the state's severe fiscal crisis.  The ASAP team completed 278 calls for assistance, and was declined in 49 incidents.

Staff victims who accepted individual crisis debriefings were 165 males (59%) and 114 women (41%).  The assault was usually unprovoked (62%) and committed during mealtimes by a male patient (56%).  These assaults most commonly involved less senior mental health workers (63%) and registered nurses (16%).  While some assaults resulted in severe physical injuries, the most common injury was bruises with swelling.  These findings are consistent with previously reported studies (Flannery et al., 1994).

Several staff victims reported symptoms of fright, anger, hypervigilance, sleep disturbance, and intrusive memories.  For most staff, these psychological sequelae associated with psychological trauma and PTSD passed within 3-10 days, and most had regained a sense of reasonable mastery (81%), had a stable network of caring attachments (91%), and were able to make some meaningful sense of why the violent event had taken place (75%).  During this period, 9% of employee victims continued to experience significant problems with syptomatology, together with disruptions in mastery, attachment, and meaning.  These findings of continuing impairment are consistent with previously published data (Caldwell, 1992).

CISD for ward communities as a whole were requested in more than half of the cases during the first 5 months of the ASAP I. As individual ASAP debriefings continued, the staff felt supported, and requests for CISD interventions decreased to less than 5% thereafter. The team leader responded to CISD requests, where CISD was clinically indicated. These included multiple assault incidents in the admission and treatment units, as well as the sudden death of a patient from cardiac arrest in the day hall, the sudden death of a patient who choked to death at lunch time, and the murder of a nurse on his way to work.

Fourteen staff victims attended the staff victims' support group for an average of 2-3 sessions per employee victim. Some recalled painful past incidents of personal victimization, including rape, incest, domestic violence, major car accidents, and previous duty-related episodes of assault that were triggered by the current patient assaults. Three staff victims were referred for professional counseling. In only one case did the family of a staff victim request short-term counseling for family members.

*ASAP II.* ASAP II responded to 125 calls for assistance from March, 1994 to August, 1995. ASAP services were accepted in 109 cases and were declined in 16 episodes.

Employee victims included 67 male staff (62%) and 42 female staff (38%). Assaults were again usually unprovoked and occurred during meal times. These assaults were committed by a female (60%) or male (40%) patient with a diagnosis of psychosis (57%) or personality disorder (17%). Assaults with bruises (33%) were the most frequent type of injury, and less senior mental health workers (90%) were again the most frequent victims of these assaults.

ASAP II employee victims reported hypervigilance, sleep disturbance, and intrusive memories as frequent symptoms. Within 3-10 days, most employee victims experienced the passing of these symptoms and the restoration of mastery (63%), attachments (68%) and a meaningful sense of why the incident had occurred (65%). However, 15% of these staff victims continued to experience significant disruptions in symptomatology, and in one or more of the three domains of basic psychological functioning.

CISD unit debriefings were utilized primarily for seriously disruptive events on patient-care sites. For example, in one instance, a thirty-year, and much loved, employee of one hospital was killed on her way to work in a car accident. The ASAP team sent ASAP members in teams of two to each unit to facilitate grief work individually and in small groups.  Finally, due to staffing limitations, each of the three ASAP team leaders had to meet informally with staff victims needing additional support.  Again, victims usually did not need more than two sessions, and no one was referred for professional counseling.

*Employee Victims Who Declined.*  ASAP I was declined in 49 episodes and ASAP II was declined in 16 incidents.

The profile of those who declined was similar in both data sets.  They were primarily less senior (80%), male (85%) mental health workers.  In ASAP I, those who declined were more likely to work the 3:30 P.M. to 11:00 P.M. shift (53%).  The most frequently stated reasons for declining ASAP were that (1) the episode was minor in nature, or (2) assaults "come with the turf."

## Declines in Assaults

An unexpected outcome of ASAP I was a sharp reduction (63%) in the frequency of assault over a twenty-two month period after ASAP I was fielded.  This decline is noted in table 1, and reflects a consistent and steady decline over these several months.  When downsizing began at point A, there was a moderate increase in patient-to-patient assaults, but no corresponding increase in patient-to-staff assaults.  During this period the assault rate declined from a baserate of 30 assaults per month when ASAP I began, to a baserate of 11 assaults per month when the hospital closed [$t$ (df = 8) = 16.47, $p<$ .005].

Table 2 illustrates a similar reduction in the assault rate (40%) in *each* of the three facilities in ASAP II.  The assault rate declined from an average baserate of 32 assaults per month for all three facilities to an average baserate of 7 per month [$F$ (4/40) = 80.85, $p <$.0001].

The reader is referred to chapter two for a discussion of the possible reasons for these declines in assaults.

## Dollar Cost Savings

The ASAP I team costs were estimated at $40,000 per year in salaried hours spent on ASAP-related duties.  (These ASAP costs are actually less because ASAP team members completed all of their regularly assigned tasks in addition to their ASAP functions.)

Prior to ASAP in facility I, an average of 15 employees left

# Table 1

## ASAP I:  Probability of Assaults at Five Month Intervals

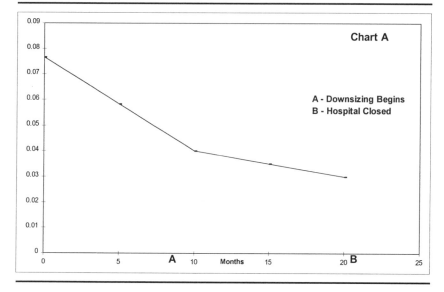

# Table 2

## ASAP II:  Probability of Assaults at Quarterly Intervals

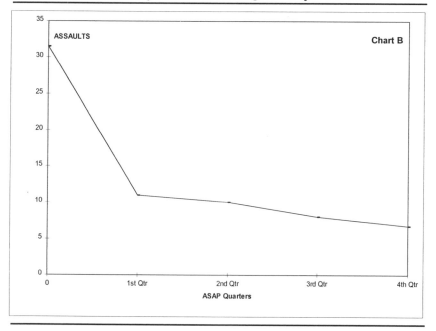

the facility for reasons related to assaults by patients. After ASAP I was fielded, only one employee left the hospital for this reason. With an ASAP team costing $40,000 per year and with an estimated replacement cost of $12,000 for an employee who was replaced, on this one outcome measure alone ASAP I paid for itself each year, and saved the facility an additional $268,000 over a two-year period.

Additional savings were also realized in both ASAP I and ASAP II because of the decline in assaults, which resulted in less medical and legal expense, less sick leave and Industrial Accident claims, and sustained productivity (Flannery et al., 1994a).

## Special Outcomes

An analysis of the ASAP I data revealed three additional outcomes of note in attempting to assess the impact of assaultive violence in the ASAP I facility: gender differences among employee victims, weak administrative leadership, and the role of ASAP I in facility safety during downsizing.

*Gender Differences Among Employee Victims.* An analysis of the ASAP I data revealed that same gender assaults (male patient/male staff, female patient/female staff) were significantly higher than gender different assaults $[x^2(1,N = 223) = 44.44, p <.001]$ (Flannery et al., 1994).

Of those employees accepting ASAP I, 165 male staff (59.9%) were assaulted by male patients in 117 episodes (71%), and by female patients in 48 incidents (29%). Male staff were assaulted in 87 apparently random acts of violence (53%), and in 78 episodes during restraint procedures (47%). Of the 114 female staff victims who accepted ASAP (41%), these female staff members were assaulted by 39 male patients (35%) and 74 female patients (65%). Female staff were more likely to be victims of random acts of violence (79 cases, 69%) than during restraint procedures (35 cases, 31%).

*Weak Administrative Leadership.* A further analysis of the ASAP I data revealed a second important finding, namely the relationship between weak administrative leadership and levels of assault. Three less well managed units had a disproportionately and continuously higher level of patient-to-staff assault rates, even as the hospital's overall assault rate was declining. Of the 327 ASAP I assaults, 176 (69%) occurred on these three units, and of the 49

ASAP I declines for assistance, 34 of these refusals (70%) occurred on these same three units (Flannery et al., 1996).

*Downsizing Safely.* In 1994, Snyder (1994) published a study that reported on large increases in the frequency of patient assaults on staff in a large state mental hospital during the years between 1980 and 1989, as the hospital census decreased due to downsizing. During this period, continuing care units were closed, previously unlocked units were locked, specialty units were closed, and the admission services were expanded. Snyder (1994) cited the admission of more disturbed patients, a decline in more healthy patients, and overcrowding with decreased security as possible contributing factors. He considered the hospital itself as an important variable affecting the increased risk of patient assaults during a period of downsizing.

An analysis of the ASAP I data with its declines in the frequency of assault demonstrate that downsizing need not necessarily result in increased risks of patient assaults on staff. The hospital can be a moderating variable to enhance safety. When the ASAP I facility was closed, clear communication about downsizing; closing admission units first; and providing specialty consult services, including ASAP, appear to have been important variables in keeping assault rates lowered (Flannery et al., 1997).

## Changing Demographics of Assaultive Inpatients

Between the years of ASAP I (1990-1992) and ASAP II (1994 to present), the state mental health authority responded to the state's fiscal crisis and the national trend toward downsizing and the privatizing of community-based services. This modified the state's health care delivery service so that the ASAP II state hospitals became primarily continuing care units. An analysis of the characteristics of assaultive inpatients prior to and after downsizing revealed dramatic changes in the inpatient population, as can be seen in table 3.

Prior to downsizing, the profile of the assaultive patient was that of a male (75%), with a diagnosis of psychosis (100%), and with histories of substance abuse (56%), violence toward others (93%), and personal victimization (41%). After downsizing, the profile reflects a shift in gender mix to more females (58%), with a diagnosis of psychosis (61%) or personality disorder (24%), and with past

# Table 3

**Characteristics of Assaultive Patients Pre/Post Downsizing:**

| Variable | Pre-Downsizing N = 96 | Post-Downsizing N = 125 |
|---|---|---|
| Gender | Male | Female |
| Diagnosis | Psychosis | Psychosis/Personality Disorder |
| Substance Abuse | 56% | 44% |
| Violence Toward Others | 93% | 88% |
| Personal Victimization | 41% | 63% |

histories of substance abuse (44%), violence toward others (88%), and personal victimization (63%) (Flannery & Penk, 1998).

It is unclear whether these changes reflect changes in violence in the society at large, or are an outcome of downsizing practices. In any case, the lesson for ASAP programs is that employees are now at risk from a differing group of assaultive patients, and these patients may well become the focus of future ASAP debriefings of employee victims.

As we conclude our review of these exciting research findings, we should note that these are the preliminary outcomes. Again, the rule for any treatment intervention is first that it do no harm. It is possible that not all ASAP interventions may prove to be helpful or at least not be helpful in all cases. Indeed, some of those who decline ASAP services may know intuitively that a debriefing may make matters worse. Others who accept services may feel worse, but may not want to report this. Research is vital in these matters, and the next generation of ASAP studies needs to include studies of the differing ASAP crisis intervention procedures as well as of individual differences in response to ASAP service delivery.

The research findings noted here have been an important quality management tool for all of the ASAP programs. They have guided our discussions about allocating services, when we have been faced with staffing shortages, and these findings have helped us to improve the services that we deliver during this difficult, transitional period in health care. The findings on the changing nature of the characteristics of these patients prone to assault has been helpful not only to ASAP team members as they conduct their interventions, but also to the system as a whole in alerting the work force to those patients who may present with an increased risk for assault.

The important lesson from chapter five and from this chapter is that quality management, including on-going formal research, should be a key component in all ASAP programs and all other CISM approaches.

## THE ASSAULTED STAFF ACTION PROGRAM (ASAP)
## SOME FINAL THOUGHTS

This completes our overview of the ASAP program. We began with studying the reason for why ASAP teams were created: to respond to the psychological needs of the victims in the aftermath of violence.

Our general review of violence considered the nature and types of crimes as well as the six most common types of assailants and the cultural, biological, sociological, and psychological risk factors that may be present as determinants to violent behavior in any particular instance. While violence may result in death, permanent disability, and medical injury, it may also result in psychological trauma and PTSD. In examining the impact of these events beyond our control, we noted that the symptoms and disruptions in mastery, attachment, and meaning that are associated with trauma and PTSD may last until death, if the victim does not receive adequate care in these matters.

Next, we outlined the ASAP program, its philosophy, its structure, and its basic services for victims, and how these services attempt to restore or foster good functioning in those very domains of mastery, attachment, and meaning that are so often shattered by violent acts.

In detail, we proceeded step-by-step through the components needed to successfully field a team: administrative support, specific facility design, selecting the team members, training those members to specific standards of performance and clinical practice guidelines, and then the steps necessary to actually start the team. Since life does not always run smoothly, we then reviewed the basic common issues and problems that ASAP has encountered and how the ASAP program has attempted to resolve these issues thus far, so that the quality of services rendered is improved.

Finally, we examined the research potential of ASAP for its own needs and as a model for other CISM approaches by examining several methodological issues and solutions that researchers in this area of inquiry may encounter. The ASAP findings were presented as an illustration, not only of the validity of the ASAP approach, but also as an example of the importance of research as a quality management tool in its own right.

Throughout these pages we have begun each chapter with an example of what victims experience. Various types of violence and all of the six types of assailants have been included in these examples to enhance the sensitivity and understanding needed by ASAP team members as they conduct their crisis intervention procedures.

The ASAP approach is flexible and can be used for different types of settings, and for providing psychological assistance in the aftermath of many different kinds of crimes. It is modular, as we have seen, so that it can be adapted for agencies depending on frequency of need for debriefings and the ability to respond to current staffing levels, when these episodes occur. ASAP should be used primarily for providing needed support to victims. While violence reduction has occurred in some facilities, this has not happened in each facility, and further research is needed to understand what factors may lead to such decreases and what role ASAP may have in these matters. Notwithstanding, facilities with ASAP programs are perceived by their employees as helpful and caring in times of distress.

The need is real. The ASAP program is efficacious and pays for itself. There are people of goodwill waiting to volunteer. A lasting tragedy would occur if the information in these pages was not put to use. We need to put aside our denial that says that it cannot happen here and our common attitude that it "comes with the turf." We are not helpless in dealing with the aftermath of violence. Our personal commitments to one another can mitigate the needless human suffering that is associated with these dreadful acts of violence. ASAP is one helpful way to begin.

# REFERENCES

American Psychiatric Association (1984). *Family therapy and psychiatry: A report of the Task Force on Family Therapy and Psychiatry.* Washington, D.C.: American Psychiatric Association.

American Psychiatric Association (1992). *Clinician safety.* Task Force Report #33. Washington, D.C.: American Psychiatric Press.

American Psychiatric Press (1994). *Diagnostic and statistical manual of mental disorders.* Fourth Edition. Washington, D.C.: American Psychiatric Association.

Antonovsky, A. (1979). *Health, stress, and coping.* San Francisco: Josey-Bass.

Blair, D. T. (1991). Assaultive behavior: Does provocation begin in the front office? *Journal of Psychosocial Nursing, 29,* 21-26.

Bouza, A. B. (1990). *The police mystique: An insider's look at cops, crime, and the criminal justice system.* New York: Plenum Publishing.

Caldwell, M. E. (1992). The incidence of PTSD among staff victims of patient violence. *Hospital and Community Psychiatry, 43,* 838-839.

Davis, S. (1991). Violence in psychiatric inpatients: A review. *Hospital and Community Psychiatry, 42,* 585-589.

Dobrin, A., Wiersema, B., Loftin, C., and McDowall, D. (1996). *Statistical handbook of violence in America.* Phoenix: Ornyx Press.

Durkheim, E. (Trans. 1951). *Suicide: A study in sociology.* Spaulding, J. & Simpson, G. New York: The Free Press.

Everly, G. S., Jr., & Mitchell, J. T. (1997). *Critical Incident Stress Management (CISM): A new era and standard of care in crisis prevention.* Ellicott City, MD: Chevron Publishing Corporation.

Everly, G. S., Jr., & Lating, J. M. (1995). *Psychotraumatology: Key papers and core concepts in post-traumatic stress.* New York: Plenum Press.

Falsetti, S. A., Resnick, H. S., Kilpatrick, D. G., & Freedy, J. R. (1994). A review of the "Potential Stressful Events Interview": A comprehensive assessment instrument of high and low magnitude stressors. *The Behavior Therapist, 17,* 66-67.

Flannery, R. B., Jr. (1984). Religious values as a moderate variable of life stress. *Journal of Pastoral Counseling, 19,* 68-74.

Flannery, R. B., Jr. (1990, 1994). *Becoming Stress-Resistant through the project SMART program.* New York: Continuum Press.

Flannery, R. B., Jr. (1992, 1994). *Post-Traumatic Stress Disorder: The victim's guide to healing and recovery.* New York: Crossroad Press.

Flannery, R. B., Jr. (1995). *Violence in the workplace.* New York: Crossroad Press.

Flannery, R. B., Jr. (1997). *Violence in America: Coping with drugs, distressed families, inadequate schooling, and acts of hate.* New York: Continuum Publishing.

Flannery, R. B., Jr. (1998). The Assaulted Staff Action Program (ASAP): Common issues in fielding a team. *Psychiatric Quarterly,* 69: 135-142.

Flannery, R. B., Jr., Fulton, P., Tausch, J., & De Loffi, A. (1991). A program to help staff cope with psychological sequelae of assaults by patients. *Hospital and Community Psychiatry*, 42, 935-938.

Flannery, R. B., Jr., Perry, J. D., & Harvey, M. R. (1993). A structural stress-reduction group approach modified for victims of psychological trauma. *Psychotherapy, 30,* 646-650.

Flannery, R. B., Jr., Hanson, M. A., & Penk, W. E. (1994). Risk factors for psychiatric inpatient assaults on staff. *Journal of Mental Health Administration, 21,* 24-31.

Flannery, R. B., Jr., Hanson, M. A., Penk, W. E., & Flannery, G. J. (1994). Violence against women: Psychiatric patient assaults on female staff. *Professional Psychology: Research and Practice, 25,* 182-184.

Flannery, R. B., Jr., Hanson, M. A., & Penk, W. E. (1995). Patients' threats: Expanding definition of assaults. *General Hospital Psychiatry, 17,* 451-453.

Flannery, R. B., Jr., Hanson, M. A., & Penk, W. E., Flannery, G. J. & Gallagher, C. (1995). The Assaultive Staff Action Program (ASAP): An approach to coping with the aftermath of violence in the workplace. In Murphy, L. R., Hurrell, J. J., Jr., Sauter, S. L., & Keita, G. P. (Eds.), *Job stress intervention: Current practices and future directions.* Vol. III, pp. 189-212. Washington, D.C.: American Psychological Association.

Flannery, R. B., Jr., Hanson, M. A., & Penk, W. E. (1996). Program evaluation of an intervention for staff assaulted by patients. *Journal of Traumatic Stress, 9,* 317-324.

Flannery, R. B., Jr., Hanson, M. A., Penk, W. E., & Flannery, G. J. (1996). The Assaulted Staff Action Program (ASAP): Guidelines for fielding a team. In Vandenbos, G. R., & Bulatao, E. R. (Eds.), *Violence on the job: Identifying risks and developing solutions.* Pp. 327-341. Washington, D.C.: American Psychological Association.

Flannery, R. B., Jr., Hanson, M. A., Penk, W. E., Pastva, G. J., Navon, M. A., & Flannery, G. J. (1997). Hospital downsizing and patients' assaults on staff. *Psychiatric Quarterly, 68,* 67-76.

Flannery, R. B., Jr., Hanson, M. A., Penk, W. E., Goldfinger, S., Pastva, G. J., & Navon, M. A. (1998). Replicated declines in assault rates after implementation of the Assaulted Staff Action Program. *Psychiatric Services, 49*: 241-243.

Flannery, R. B., Jr., & Penk, W. E. (1998) The Practicing Psychologist and the Assaultive Psychiatric Patient. Cambridge, MA: Department of Psychiatry, The Cambridge Hospital. Manuscript submitted for publication.

Grinker, R. R., & Spiegel, J. P., (1945). *Men under stress.* New York: McGraw-Hill.

Hanson, R. H., & Balk, J. A. (1992). A replication of staff injuries in a state hospital. *Hospital and Community Psychiatry, 43,* 836-838.

Hersen, M., & Barlow, D. F. (1976). *Single-case experimental designs: Strategies for studying behavioral change.* New York: Pergammon Press.

Hinkle, L. E., & Wolfe, H. G. (1958). Ecological investigations of the relationship between illness, life experiences, and the social environment. *Annals of Internal Medicine, 49,* 1373-1378.

Horowitz, M. (1976). *Stress response syndromes.* 2nd Edition. Northvale, NJ: Aronson.

Horowitz, M. J., Vilner, N., & Alvarez, W. (1978). The Impact of Event Scale: A measure of subjective distress. *Psychosomatic Medicine, 41,* 209-218.

Hunter, M., & Carmel, H. (1992). The cost of staff injuries from inpatient violence. *Hospital and Community Psychiatry, 43,* 586-588.

Kelling, G. L., & Coles, C. M. (1996). *Fixing broken windows: Restoring order and reducing crime in our communities.* New York: Free Press.

Kenardy, J. A., Webster, R. A., Lewis, T. J., Carr, V. J., Hazell, P. L., & Carter, G. L. (1996). Stress debriefing and patterns of recovery following a natural disaster. *Journal of Traumatic Stress, 9,* 37-49.

Khantzian, E. (1985). The self-medication hypothesis of addictive disorders: Focus on heroin and cocaine. *American Journal of Psychiatry, 142,* 1259-1264.

Lindemann, E. (1944). Symptomatology and management of acute grief. *American Journal of Psychiatry, 101,* 141-148.

Lion, J. R., Snyder, W., & Merrill, G. L. (1981). Underreporting of assaults on staff in a state hospital. *Hospital and Community Psychiatry, 32,* 497-498.

Maddi, S. R. & Kobasa, S. C. (1984). *The hardy executive: Health under stress.* Homewood, IL: Dow-Jones-Irwin.

McCann, L., & Pearlman, L. A. (1990). *Psychological trauma and the adult survivor: Theory, therapy, and transformation.* New York: Brunner/Mazel.

Mitchell, J. T. (1983). When disaster strikes .... The Critical Incident Stress Debriefing process. *Journal of Emergency Medical Services*, 8, 36-39.

Mitchell, J. T., & Everly, G. S., Jr. (1996). *Critical Incident Stress Debriefing (CISD): An operations manual for the prevention of traumatic stress among emergency services and disaster workers.* 2nd Edition Revised. Ellicott City, MD: Chevron Publishing Corporation.

Morrison, E. F. (1989). Theoretical model to predict violence in hospitalized psychiatric patients. *Research on Nursing Health*, 12, 31-40.

Norris, D. (1990). *Violence against social workers: The implications for practice with the University of Sussex national research study by Carol Kedmond.* Pp. 24-40. London: Kingsley Publisher.

Norris, F. H. (1992). Epidemiology of trauma: Frequency and impact of potentially traumatic events on different demographic groups. *Journal of Consulting and Clinical Psychology, 60,* 409-418.

Occupational Safety and Health Administration (1996). *Guidelines for preventing workplace violence for health care and social service workers.* #3148. Washington, D.C.: Occupational Safety and Health Administration Publications Office.

Reid, W. H., Bollinger, M. F., & Edwards, J. G. (1989). Serious assaults by inpatients. *Psychosomatics, 30,* 54-56.

Sandoval, J. (1985). Crisis counseling: Conceptualization and general principles. *School Psychology Review, 14,* 257-265.

Starkey, D., Di Leone, H., & Flannery, R. B. Jr. (1995). Stress management for patients in a state hospital setting. *American Journal of Orthopsychiatry, 65,* 446-450

Walton, M. (1986). *The Deming management method.* New York: Perigee Books.

Wekesser, C. (1995). *Violence in the media: Current controversies.* San Diego: Greenhaven Press.

Widom, C. (1992). Does violence beget violence? A critical examination of the literature. *Psychological Bulletin, 106,* 3-38.

Winer, B. J. (1992). *Statistical principles in experimental design.* New York: McGraw-Hill.

Yalom, I. D. (1970). *The theory and practice of group psychotherapy.* New York: Basic Books.

# About the Author

Raymond B. Flannery, Jr., Ph.D., F.A.P.M., a licensed clinical psychologist, is Associate Clinical Professor of Psychology, Department of Psychiatry, Harvard Medical School in Boston, and Adjunct Assistant Professor of Psychiatry, University of Massachusetts Medical School, Worcester. For over thirty years he has been a counselor and professional educator of business persons, professionals, health care providers, and the general public about life stress, psychological trauma, and violence in the community and in the workplace. He has lectured nationally, and is the author of over sixty papers in medical and science journals.

Dr. Flannery is also the author of four books for interested professionals and the general public. *Becoming Stress-Resistant through the Project SMART Program* (New York: Continuum, 1990, and Crossroad, 1994) is for those interested in learning how to cope effectively with the general stress of life. It is based on a twelve year study of 1,200 persons and how the most adaptive among them coped with life stress. His second book, *Post-Traumatic Stress Disorder: The Victim's Guide to Healing and Recovery* (New York: Crossroad, 1992, 1994), is the first book written for victims of psychological trauma, and outlines effective coping strategies for persons seeking to recover from the severe stress of traumatic events. *Violence in the Workplace* (New York: Crossroad, 1995) is his third book, and the first to examine the general nature and causes of work-site violence. It presents a threefold approach to reduce the risk of its occurrence and to contain its aftermath, when it does occur. His fourth book, *Violence in America: Coping with Drugs, Distressed Families, Inadequate Schooling, and Acts of Hate,* is the first comprehensive review of the theories of the causes of violence, and the first to present a basic overview of what business, government, families, schools, and religion can do to stop its spread.

Dr. Flannery and his wife live in the suburbs of Boston.